The Big Bird Race

This is the story of 'The *Country Life* Record Birdwatch' on 14th May 1983.

In 1980 David Tomlinson of *Country Life* magazine led a four-man team of birdwatchers in a race to record as many species as possible in twenty-four frantic hours. A year later, a rival team from the Fauna and Flora Preservation Society challenged the *Country Life* foursome, which beat them off by a mere three species – and established a new British record in the process. In 1982 the *Country Life* team triumphed yet again with 153 species.

In this book of the 1983 Race, both sides kept a 'crow-by-crow' account of their day's birding. DAVID TOMLINSON for *Country Life* traces his team's progress; then BILL ODDIE reports for the *ffPS* team.

By comparing and contrasting the two synchronous stories, the reader is drawn into the excitement of the Race, and can follow the shifting fortunes of both teams in a way in which the contestants themselves could not!

Frontispiece, the teams in action. *Top*, the *ffPS* team: *left to right* Bill Oddie, John Gooders, Cliff Waller and Tim Inskipp (*Photo P. R. Crabb*). *Bottom*, the *Country Life* team: *left to right* Jeremy Sorensen, Peter Smith, David Tomlinson and Bill Urwin (*Photo Steve Piotrowski*)

The Big Bird Race

Bill Oddie and David Tomlinson

Foreword by Dr Roger Tory Peterson

Introduction by John Gooders

Illustrations by Laurel Tucker

COLLINS

8 Grafton Street, London W1

William Collins Sons & Co Ltd
London · Glasgow · Sydney
Auckland · Toronto · Johannesburg

First published 1983

ISBN 0 00 219053 2 Paperback
ISBN 0 00 219055 9 Hardback

Filmset by Ace Filmsetting Ltd, Frome, Somerset
Made and printed in Great Britain by
William Collins Sons & Co Ltd, Glasgow

In the interests of the well-being of certain rare species
particularly susceptible to disturbance, some of the sites
mentioned in this book have either been given invented
names or have not been named at all.

Contents

Foreword

ROGER TORY PETERSON

THIS FOREWORD IS A REPORT from the erstwhile colonies, where bird-spotting and listing on the competitive level has a history that goes back more than half a century. Prior to that, the shotgun school of ornithology prevailed. Audubon, who with Alexander Wilson started it all in America, inferred that it was not a really good day unless he shot at least a hundred birds.

My dear friend, the late James Fisher, once commented that the observation of birds can be many things. It can be a science, an art, a recreation, a tradition – or a bore – depending on the observer. He might have added, 'a game or a sport', for that is exactly what most birding or listing is.

Some seventy years ago, when the star of the field-glass fraternity was rising and it was no longer necessary to check every observation over the sights of a shotgun, some fellow with good legs, good ears, and sharp eyes found he could list 100 species of birds in a day. I know of at least three such lists prior to 1916; two in New York State and one in Ohio. As early as 1930, Charles Urner and his party ran up a total of 162 species in a single day in New Jersey. Since then such totals have become commonplace.

An all-out tournament, usually staged in mid-May when spring migration is at flood-tide, was something I had not heard of before I came into contact with the birders of the big cities along the east coast of the United States in the late 1920s. New Yorkers and Bostonians called it the 'Big Day'; Philadelphians the 'Century Run'; New Jerseyites the 'Lethal Tour'; and Washingtonians the 'Grim Grind'. One academic with a hint of arrogance dubbed it 'ornithogolfing', and

(*Photo P. R. Crabb*)

recently some of its devotees have been called 'binocular junkies'. On our side of the ocean we have not yet adopted the British terms 'twitching' or 'twitchers', nor do I think we will; although we sometimes refer to bird-listers as 'tickers'.

It was a stroke of genius when some imaginative entrepreneur saw the fund-raising possibilities, funnelling all that expertise and effort into something more tangible than the list. The name 'Birdathon' was coined and as far as I know the first one was launched in Ontario in 1977 to raise funds for the Long Point Observatory on Lake Erie. This lucrative idea was soon copied by others: Manomet Observatory in Massachusetts (1979), Point Reyes Observatory in California (1980), the Gull Island Project of the Linnaean Society of New York (1980), and on a national level by the National Audubon Society, the American counterpart of the RSPB, in 1981.

Because of my long ties with the Audubon I was chosen to be National Chairman of the event. There would be various teams in different parts of the country. I decided to make my own count on the upper Texas coast, famous for its fall-outs of migrants crossing the Gulf of Mexico. That effort on 25th April 1981 was an endurance test that I will long remember. Our total was 184 species, well short of the 'Big Day' record for the upper Texas coast which stood at 193, but inasmuch as $90 had been pledged by my sponsors for each bird, more than $16,000 were added to the coffers of the Audubon Society.

However, in 1972 a team of super-stars had amassed a one-day total of 226 species in Texas by combining the Rio Grande Valley and the upper Texas coast and by observing no speed laws.

Victor Emanuel who had planned our own strategy and logistics reasoned that the only way to surpass that record of ten years' standing was to fly between the Rio Grande and the upper coast, thereby saving five hours; so in 1982 we set our date for Tuesday 27th April. To help us, Victor recruited the best eyes and ears in Texas – John Rowlett, who teaches judo to the Texas National Guard and recently got his PhD on the English poets, and Ted Parker who holds the world record for a 'Big Day' – 330 species at Explorers Inn in Peru.

After a midnight 'breakfast' near the Mexican border we listened to identifiable migrants in the night sky before proceeding upriver in our van. We made numerous stops, cupping our ears for rails, owls, and other night birds which responded to our tapes. As the sun rose in the morning sky our list was further augmented by Mexican specialties in the mesquite forests along the river and desert birds in the arid brush.

At 10.00, when we reached the airfield at Falcon Dam, three small planes awaited us; one for the four birders, a second for the press, and a third for the television crew. After a two-hour flight to the upper Texas coast, we landed on a makeshift airstrip on the Bolivar Peninsula. The tides were just right for waders and the oases on the barrier beaches were dripping with migration-weary warblers, thrushes, tanagers, and orioles.

Our day finished with 235. When we broke out the champagne at 20.00 to celebrate we still had a chance for three or four marsh birds before midnight, but the frog chorus was so deafening that we could hear no responses to our tapes. But we had broken the continental record of 231, made in California the year before.

California has always been very competitive with Texas, so when I agreed to take on the 1983 'Birdathon' I thought I should give the opposition a chance – using planes. We put things in the hands of Don Roberson, the scholarly author of *Rare Birds of the West Coast*. Don, a genius at organisation, chose four of the sharpest field birders in California for our team of six: Dr Laurence Binford, Dr Jeri Langhorn, and Dr Michael Parmenter and his son John.

Things did not look promising the day before when we flew our small plane from Monterey to Yuma on the Mexican border, braving strong winds and driving rain as we cleared the desert ranges. But the weather took a turn for the better, and before dawn we were able to stimulate four species of rail and both bitterns with our tapes. From the lower Colorado River we flew to Salton Sea, a vast expanse of saline water below sea level where thousands of waders, gulls, terns, grebes, and pelicans congregate to feed on the swarming brine shrimp. We missed the best bird of the day, a Spotted Redshank in full breeding plumage, which

The use of tape-recorders to play the sound of a bird, to stimulate a bird of the same species to 'answer', is prohibited in the 'Big Bird Race' (see p. 19).

put in its appearance after we left. It was the first record for California. Birders from far and near came to see this Eurasian wader during the following days.

The reporter from the *Los Angeles Times*, who covered the story, wrote:

'With the tension of the final day of a major golf tournament, the pace of a forced march led by a demented basic-training drill sergeant and a sense of the absurd that might captivate an avant-garde comedian, the World Series of birdwatching was played in California during the weekend. The National Audubon Society's annual Birdathon, in which a team of world-class competitive birders rush around a state trying to identify as many different species as possible in a 24-hour period was as significant in its own way as the World Series or the Super Bowl . . . as significant in its own way as a 21-foot pole vault.'

As the weather closed in, our final flight was to Monterey and the coast. To break the record we literally had to add a new bird every four minutes. When darkness fell we were still two or three short. By luck a pair of Canada Geese that had been staked out the day before were spotted in the headlights of our car. Later, by playing our tapes in the cloud-shrouded mountains, we finally got responses from a Saw-whet Owl and a Spotted Owl. We had made it – 236! But, according to the rules set down by the American Birding Association we fell short by one bird. The rules specify that a 'Big Day' party should stay together at all times (we did) and that 95% of the birds must be seen or heard by everyone in the group. Our percentage was 94.9. One bird had to be lopped off!

The official score was 235 this year for California; 235 last year for Texas. A real cliff-hanger.

There was no overtime period.

I welcome this book which describes how our British cousins have conducted their own all-out birding tournaments. The idea of two teams competing with each other over the same terrain on the same day is a new twist. I wish them good weather and lucky breaks in their future bird races where records are certain to be broken.

ROGER TORY PETERSON

Introduction

JOHN GOODERS

IT WAS, IF MEMORY SERVES ME correctly, in the Star and Garter in Poland Street that the idea of a challenge match between *Country Life* and the *Fauna and Flora Preservation Society* was first put to me. A team from *Country Life* had just set a record for the number of birds seen in Britain in a day and a challenge seemed inevitable. At that time the 'Star and Garter' was the watering hole of a number of conservation and environmental organisations that existed in temporary and borrowed hovels nearby; and in any case Sam, the landlord, served a particularly fine pint by Soho standards. The *dramatis personae* were: bearded John Burton, Executive Secretary of the *ffPS*; Tim Inskipp, member of the TRAFFIC team investigating the trade in rare and endangered wildlife; and Robbie Chapman former television PA, but by then converted to the wildlife cause; and myself.

John ('Jumping John' to his friends) had already challenged *Country Life*'s David Tomlinson to a sort of 'America's Cup' of birding – a one-day test of daring, skill and endurance that involved seeing which team could spot the maximum number of bird species in a single day. The challenge had – foolishly, we thought – been accepted, and Jumping John was busily recruiting ornitho-mercenaries to fight on behalf of the *ffPS*.

He had, he told me, already recruited one goodie. Diminutive, bearded Bill Oddie had agreed to join the merry band. Bill would, of course, attract the media, and their interest was crucial if we were to get the sort of publicity we needed. I should add at this point that the whole purpose of the challenge, soon to become the '*Country Life* Record Birdwatch' and the 'Big Bird

Race', was to attract sponsorship and thus raise cash for bird charities. In enlisting the participation of Bill Oddie, John had got not only a television personality, but the only birder-celebrity living in Britain today.

Tim Inskipp had himself already been recruited because of his involvement in conservation and because he has one of the best pairs of birding ears in the country. In such company, how could we go wrong? . . . and I readily agreed to join the team as driver, fund-raiser, publicity manager and writer of bits and pieces including the introduction to this (as then unmooted) book.

By sheer good fortune (as they say in books) I was able to enlist the aid of Robbie to help me in these multifarious activities and she readily (as they say in books) agreed to join the team as non-playing fund-raiser and publicity manager, and effectively leave me as a sort of ornitho-chauffeur.

Then, just as it seemed that we had got our world-beating team together, John dropped the bombshell. He would not, he stated, be a member of the team himself. Rather he would act as a non-playing captain, remaining in the background to help pull things together and plan for our eventual success. After what seemed like minutes of debate, but which actually must have lasted several seconds, we reluctantly agreed. We knew we were losing a fine mammalogist and one of the select number of ornithologists who have actually added a new bird to the British list – Bobolink, Isles of Scilly, September 1962. Keeping stiff upper lips and choking back the emotion we begged him to reconsider. But even a further seventeen (or was it two?) pints did not produce a chink in this iron man's armour.

I have always admired John's unique ability to think up things for other people to do, and it was good to know that he would be behind us all the way. Some have suggested that John is a megalomaniac; but everyone who meets him soon realises that under the innocent exterior lurks a power-crazy fanatic. As ever, it was John who had thought the whole thing through – the fourth man would be Cliff Waller, my old chum from the Suffolk coast. Cliff is the warden of a string of nature reserves covering some of the richest birding country in Britain. His local knowledge and identification skills would be invaluable to the team. What's more, he had a particularly good working relationship with the landlords of 'The Fox' at Shadingfield that might prove invaluable in an emergency. So there we were: Bill Oddie, Tim Inskipp, Cliff Waller and John Gooders. What a team! . . . intelligence, knowledge, skill, field-craft, personality, perseverance, good taste, determination, stamina, willpower and rugged good looks all combined in four modest and humble individuals. What could *Country Life* put up against us?

First they had David Tomlinson, a sort of squire-like figure best known for his penchant for amazingly fast cars, and Assistant Editor of *Country Life* magazine. It had been David's original idea to set up the *Country Life* Record Birdwatch on a sponsored basis, and the previous year he and his merry men had established a new British record of 132 in the day and raised over £1,000 for the Royal Society of the Protection of Birds (RSPB). The 'Big Day' was not an original idea, but it was David who turned a bit of fun into the sponsored event that was to become the 'Big Bird Race'.

The *Country Life* team relied for their local knowledge on Jeremy Sorenson, warden of the RSPB's famous Minsmere Reserve and one of only a handful of un-bearded nature reserve wardens in the country. If any reserve could lay claim to offering a home to the greatest variety of birds it would be Minsmere. So in enlisting Jeremy the opposition had got themselves a head start.

Their third member was Peter Smith, of whom frankly hardly anyone had actually heard. Was Peter a secret weapon? A genius at unmasking awkward warblers, perhaps? Word filtered through that he had spent long periods of time in the Middle East and rumours of his expertise with transitional-plumaged waders were rife. However, one nameless wag suggested that, being less than a giant, Peter had been included in the team as one of the few birders who would actually fit into the back seat of the Porsche that David Tomlinson insisted on using. Eventually the truth came out – Peter Smith had been involved in every 'Big Day' in Suffolk since 1957 and was co-holder of the British 'Big Day' record.

Their fourth man was Bill Urwin, a schoolteacher from Acle in Norfolk and a man with his ear very much to the ground as far as East Anglian rarities go. By sheer good fortune Bill is bearded – the idea of a team of birders without a beard seems quite unthinkable – so in this respect alone he was an ideal complement to the rest of the team.

Country Life had, then, gathered together a team of highly qualified birdmen that would form stiff opposition to the *ffPS*. What they lacked in handsomeness and modesty they more than compensated for in athletic ability – a factor that was, in the end, to prove vital.

The idea of a 'Big Day' was not, as I have said, completely original. For all we know, Aristotle (who was something of a twitcher in his own right) had knocked up a considerable day-list in and around Athens some 2,400 years ago. However, modern 'Big Days' began in the early 1950s when a small Suffolk team had managed 106 in the twenty-four hours. The fact had been reported by the BBC more as a curiosity than anything else, but it was sufficient to inspire two Suffolk schoolboys into action in 1957.

Twitcher: one whose aim is to see as many different bird species as possible in a day, or a year, or a lifetime.

On May Day of that year youthful Peter Smith and David Pearson set out at 05.15 on their bikes to beat the record. Choosing the Walberswick area they knew so well they worked their total up to 85 by breakfast time at 10.30. Bird number 45 had been a Sparrowhawk and, as Peter recounts, 'If you get a Sparrowhawk, then it's worth going on'. Along the way they had taken in Minsmere, but only from the public hide along the shore. At that time this fabulous reserve could only be visited with permits booked in advance and strictly limited in number. So they had made the best they could of the free views and then moved on across the River Blyth to a little gem of a place called Buss Creek near Southwold.

Sparrowhawk

At this time Buss Creek was one of the best wader sites along the Suffolk coast, though, alas, it was soon to be drained, and is now only poor grazing for a few cattle and sheep. By mid-afternoon their score had crept up to 98 and a Garganey just before teatime brought them to 106 and equal to the record. A hard-pedalled dash down the coast to Snape produced Avocet – there were none at Minsmere at that time – and the record was broken. A Long-eared Owl obliged soon afterwards and Peter's log contains reference to something that he quaintly called 'Brown Owl' in the idiom of the 1950s and which was bird number 111. Try as they may the duo could not cycle fast enough to get to Sibton before dark and thus dipped out on that great Suffolk rarity of the time – Canada Goose. By 22.30 they were back in Blythburgh having covered 80 miles and happy with their 111 total.

Looking over their list it is interesting to note the differences between the birds seen in 1957 and those seen in the early 1980s. Canada Goose apart, Peter and David missed Collared Dove, at that time an exceptional rarity confined to a couple of spots in Norfolk, but now so common as to be a pest in some areas. They also failed to see Cetti's and Savi's Warblers, then unknown in Britain, as well as Greylag and Egyptian Geese which had not become established as feral breeding birds in 1957. Black Redstarts were still more or less confined to the bombed sites of London and thus similarly unavailable to the lads; but they managed to miss both Fulmar and Kittiwake, birds they probably should have got.

Feral: formerly a captive species, whose population is now self-supporting in the wild.

In contrast, Grey Partridge, which is now an awkward bird to see in Suffolk, was easily found and ticked off as bird number 11 on their list. Stone Curlew, Woodlark, Whinchat and Stonechat all fell without difficulty, whereas the 1980s teams have always had to work very hard to get these increasingly scarce birds. In 1957, and for several years thereafter, a pair of Corn Buntings bred just outside Westleton on the Minsmere road. But the species was always highly localised and when this pair disappeared another problem bird was created.

The next attempt on the 'Big Day' record took place the following year on 24th May. Once again Peter and David spent the whole day on bikes, but it was too late in the season and many of the migrants had already passed through on their way north, and only 108 species were ticked off. At this time 108 was the second highest total ever, but was nevertheless a great disappointment. Birds included Montagu's Harrier and both Canada and Greylag Geese, the latter a life bird for Peter.

An attempt to compensate, and, incidentally, to see if the autumn season might actually be better, was made on 9th August 1958. Though 87 species were seen before breakfast, Peter and David had to be content with a total of 107. With so many birds not singing they inevitably missed a number of woodland species and, though passage waders were better, the balance did not work out in favour of this season. To our knowledge 107 remains the UK autumn best – but we shall probably soon hear to the contrary.

Still schoolboys in Leiston, Peter and David were on their bikes once more on 10th May 1959. This time they had got the date right and with the experience of three previous attempts behind them they were up and at it by 03.30. They kicked off with the elusive Long-eared Owl and were up to 57 within the first two hours. By 06.30 they had reached 70 and the century came up at 09.00. This remarkable total exactly parallels that achieved by the *ffPS* team in 1982, though well behind the insomniac *Country Life* team's effort of 06.22 the same year.

However at this point Pete and Dave took time off for breakfast and did not get started again until 10.30. This remarkably civilised, indeed gentlemanly, approach to the 'Big Day' was not to feature in Peter's later association with the *Country Life* team, though we of the *ffPS* have always felt that one's enthusiasm should be kept in its place, and have invariably sojourned for a leisurely repast at this sensible hour. But I digress.

Having invested an hour in refreshment, our school-boy heroes passed on to 110 by mid-day, having located the regular Red-backed Shrike and an unusual (for Suffolk) singing Wood Warbler. Thereafter, and with the record clearly in their sights, Pete and Dave struggled through a frustrating early afternoon pedalling from one spot to the next without adding a single new bird. Then at Easton Broad a Black-tailed Godwit brought them to 112 and a new UK record.

Now Pete and Dave brought their secret weapon into play, and modern high technology entered the 'Big Day' scene for the first time. Back at Blythburgh the French mistress and her car awaited the arrival of our two stalwarts. Just how Miss Hawtin, for it was she, had been persuaded by two Leiston School sixth-formers to join this bizarre exercise remains a well-kept secret – a secret that discretion has prevented my investigating further. Not for me the sensational disclosures of the gutter press. No 'Shock-Horrors' or 'French mistress takes Schoolboys on Suffolk bird rampage'.

Anyway, armed with the speed of an upright 1950svintage Ford Escort the lads were up to 118 by 18.00 and finished with a Stone Curlew at 21.30 for a grand total of 120.

It was not until 16th May 1964 that the obsessive lads were together again for another try. Despite being motorised and picking up goodies such as Ferruginous Duck, Red-breasted Merganser and the by then more widespread Collared Dove, they finished the day with another total of 120 species. For the first time they missed Woodlark – a sign of the times, that! – as well as Kingfisher and Barn Owl.

The following year saw Pete and Dave at it once more on 13th May 1965. Long before the first Skylark began to sing they had ticked off Long-eared Owl, Water Rail, Bittern and the inevitable Tawny Owl and by 07.00 87 species had fallen. Once more Minsmere produced a rush of species, but as ever Pete and Dave were confined to the public hides. They worked their way northward along the coast, putting the temptation to dash to the Brecks and the Norfolk coast firmly aside, and by lunch a total of 117 species had been amassed. Even so they had not seen a Magpie in this well-keepered area, and even a Kestrel had not been forthcoming. Eventually the Magpie as well as Woodlark, Short-eared Owl and, after twelve hours in the field, a Kestrel fell to their binoculars. Tea-time, and 124 birds was a new record, and still with a little daylight to use. An early Nightjar, a Stone Curlew, and a total of 126 was set as a new UK record.

Soon afterwards both Peter and David took posts abroad, and the 'Big Day' faded from the scene. There were rumours of a Scottish team having had a go at the record; but to all intents and purposes the 126 in East Suffolk remained the record until 1980.

Peter Smith had by then returned from his Middle East oil jaunt and settled near Sevenoaks in Kent. There, at the famed Sevenoaks Gravel Pit reserve created by the late Jeffrey Harrison, he had met an earnest young birdwatcher called David Tomlinson who was keen to have a bash at the 126 record. Together they planned their campaign and enlisted the aid of Jeremy Sorenson at Minsmere to act as adjudicator. No doubt it would have all been a lot of fun had they not hit on the idea of trying to gather sponsors to raise money for the RSPB. At that point David's

Collared Dove

journalistic connections came into play and the '*Country Life* Sponsored Birdwatch' was born.

The work that David and his wife Janet put into the campaign to raise funds paid off and, in the event, £1,200 went to the RSPB's 'Silver Meadows Appeal'. In addition David managed to borrow an eye-catching Porsche 924 from Porsche (GB) to act as a sort of high-speed hoarding for sponsors' stickers and incidentally to satisfy, albeit temporarily, his craving for fast cars.

Armed with two excellent team-mates David Tomlinson was about to set off in pursuit of the 126 British record when David Pearson reappeared on the scene. On leave from Kenya he was quickly recruited to the team and the foursome set off at 03.50 on the 10th May 1980. By their own standards in years to follow, this was a particularly modest starting time; but they were up to 31 species by the time the sun rose at 05.00. Interestingly enough the second bird of the day had been the Canada Goose that had proved so elusive to David Pearson and Peter Smith some twenty years earlier. By 08.09 the 100 came up with a reeling Grasshopper Warbler while Redwing, Fieldfare, Pintail, Ring Ousel and Mediterranean Gull had all been ticked off along with the newly colonising Cetti's Warbler. This resident warbler had first bred in Britain early in 1972 following a sensational spread northwards across Europe. It was a bird that the Pearson/Smith duo could never have expected to see during their schoolboy peregrinations around Suffolk, though by 1980 close on 200 pairs were breeding at nearly 50 different sites in southern and eastern England.

Canada Goose

Moving northwards the quartet picked up diving duck and grebes, always difficult species groups in East Suffolk, at Benacre and were rewarded by spotting a Caspian Tern offshore. Surprisingly enough this is the only really rare bird that has been discovered on any of the recent birdwatches – though it was subsequently rejected by the Rarities Committee who judge such things. The *ffPS* team has often debated, with mock seriousness, what it would do if an outstanding rarity were to be discovered during the 'Big Bird Race'. Such a bird would require full field-notes by every member of the team in order to gain full authenticity, and that would be a considerable time-wasting effort. Fortunately, or unfortunately, the occasion has yet to arise, though a Little Stint in some strange intermediate plumage on the beach at Minsmere caused a few hearts to flutter in 1981.

At 15.30 the record of 126 was equalled, but, as the bird was a flamingo with green legs and pink 'knees' and obviously a Chilean Flamingo that had flown away from a wildfowl collection, it did not count. Twenty-nine agonising minutes later a Woodlark was ticked off at a regular spot without the team leaving the car. The time was 15.59 and the record had been equalled. It took another 50 minutes to beat it, but then a Short-eared Owl was collected at Orford and slowly the list was built up to 133 with a Woodcock roding at Walberswick at 20.48. Eliminating the flamingo, a new record of 132 had been set. Once more the team had not left East Suffolk.

The following weekend David Pearson joined up with his future replacement Bill Urwin and Norfolk-based Bryan Bland to record 138 species. The trio had, however, started in Suffolk and ended in Norfolk so there was a pointer for the future to the *Country Life* team. This trio missed the 'easy' Green Woodpecker, but managed to pick up Shore Lark, Bluethroat and Velvet Scoter – good birds for mid-May. Soon afterwards RSPB Scottish representative and ex-warden of Fair Isle Bird Observatory, Roy Dennis met up with Roger Broad to set a Scottish record of 130 species on 31st May. And so the scene was set for that historic meeting in the 'Star and Garter' in London's Soho.

In *BTO News* for October 1980 David Tomlinson had set out a proposed code of conduct for 'Big Day' listers and it was that to which the infant *ffPS* team gave its first attentions.

1. The welfare of the bird must come first, and disturbance (flushing sitting birds off nest, etc.) is not allowed.
2. Attracting birds with tape recorders is forbidden.
3. Record attempts must be made on one calendar day.
4. All members of team must see or hear each bird recorded.
5. Rarity records must be accepted by the Rarities Committee.
6. Oiled or sick birds do not count.
7. All birds counted must be on the British List, but

escapes should be noted and added in brackets.

8. Trespassing in search of birds is forbidden.

These all seemed very reasonable and have formed the basis of the event ever since. However, one of the prime functions of the 'Big Bird Race' is to raise money, and it was perfectly obvious from the moment the challenge was made that a *race* would be much more likely to attract the attention of the media than a single record attempt. The attentions of the media would in turn attract more sponsors and thus raise more money.

In talking to television, radio and newspaper people it quickly became clear that 'an event' such as the '*Country Life* Record Birdwatch' needed a finishing line and we quickly agreed upon a new Rule 9.

9. Both teams shall cross the finishing line at Blyth-burgh before 24.00 midnight.

We also agreed that it would be much better if both teams consisted of the same number of birders, and we settled on teams of four.

Thus the stage was set, and while Robbie and myself became virtually full-time fund raisers and public relations executives for the *ffPS*, David and Janet Tomlinson were busily pursuing the same functions on behalf of the *Country Life* team. We made huge lists of companies that had something, no matter how tenuous, to do with birds. We added companies with bird names, bird emblems and bird products. We listed companies past whose doors we were going to drive, whose pubs and restaurants we might use and whose food we might eat. We put down the publishers of all my books and with whom anyone of us had a connection. Then, with all the skill and nerve of a former TV PA, Robbie phoned the Managing Director of each company and asked for money.

Press releases flowed from the *Country Life* offices informing the media of the great event and every change in equipment. Once again David 'Speedy' Tomlinson had lined up a 150 m.p.h. Porsche. Soon we were equipped with an even faster 160 m.p.h. Aston Martin, courtesy of Pace Petroleum. Out went the Press Release. Then we were promised coverage by BBC Television's 'Wildtrack' programme. Out went another Press Release. Radio Orwell promised coverage throughout the day. The *Eastern Daily Press* would send a reporter, National newspapers started to print bits and pieces, and the ball was rolling.

Throughout it all we used Bill Oddie's name to open doors and gain entry to a world that is otherwise difficult to penetrate. Bill did radio, television and newspaper interviews left, right and centre, and Robbie and I became his personal PR Officers for the duration. Throughout the whole business he was marvellous and performed on demand without a single complaint.

Then, a week before 1981's 'Big Day', we had an unexpected scoop. The *Country Life* team had, it came out, spent the previous weekend on a dummy run. They had worked out their schedule down to the nearest minute and were treating the whole thing as a military operation. We, meanwhile, had been so busy arranging publicity and sponsorship that we had not even met up as a team. The contrast between the two approaches could not have been more stark and it was Bill who immediately turned this to our advantage by referring to the opposition as 'The Players' and ourselves as 'The Gentlemen'. Naturally this went down a bomb with the media and the *ffPS* team inevitably emerged as 'the stars' of any shows we did. The *Country Life* team took it all in good spirits, as we knew they would. After all, the whole idea was to generate interest, and thus cash, and Bill's gift of the gab certainly did that.

On the Friday before the 'Big Day' we all gathered in East Suffolk – the *Country Life* team at Minsmere, the *ffPS* team at Cliff Waller's charming cottage overlooking the river at Blythburgh. Suddenly we found ourselves surrounded by television crews – Anglia Television sent a news crew from Norwich, and we had great satisfaction in seeing ourselves on the box later that evening. Meanwhile BBC's 'Wildtrack' attempted to obtain a schedule of our movements similar to the one David had supplied for the *Country Life* opposition. All in vain – we simply didn't have one.

Cliff's sitting room became an improvised television studio with cameras and microphones everywhere and miles of cable running in virtually every direction. Then a nice chap called Daragh Croxson from Radio Orwell turned up to do some interviews prior to 'the off'. By no coincidence at all Daragh turned out to be a keen birder and it was great to work with someone who understood birds and our problems. Robbie's carefully arranged PR schedule was torn to shreds as we attempted to be in three places at once and satisfy all the needs of the various operations. Then, just as it seemed that we had finally got it all sorted out, the 'phone rang and the cultured tones of Angus McGill of the London *Evening Standard* inquired whether he could join us for the day.

Not wishing to be discouraging, I informed said Mr McGill that we would be starting at 03.00, driving a 160 m.p.h. car flat out for 1,000 miles, and that there certainly wasn't a spare seat for him. Undaunted he arranged to meet us for breakfast on the 'Big Day'.

'Early to bed' seemed a good idea and with not more than a passing thought of the enemy we turned in. At 03.00 alarm-bells rang and bleary-eyed we grabbed coffee/tea/toast (delete as necessary) and were off. Our super-fast Aston Martin was left in the yard as we set out in a battered old Land Rover more suitable to our early morning plans. Nevertheless, Cliff drove with skill and daring along muddy tracks into the heart of deepest Suffolk at times reaching a staggering 50 m.p.h. We stopped to listen for Long-eared Owl, the one bird that every successful 'Big Bird Race' needs early in the day. Not a sound. Daragh appeared out of the dark with the news that the *Country Life* team had just returned from the seabird cliffs of Yorkshire. Yorkshire? Yes, *Yorkshire*! Unbeknown to us the Porsche-equipped quartet had slunk away in the early evening and armed with an expensive image-intensifier (a sort of night

The *Country Life* team in 1981: *left to right* Peter Smith, David Tomlinson, Bill Urwin and Jeremy Sorensen (*Photo Janet Tomlinson*)

viewing monocular) they had started ticking at midnight. At 00.01 a.m. they had knocked off Gannet, Guillemot, Razorbill and Kittiwake while we were still knocking out the z-z-z-z's. By 00.22 they had six species in the bag and were zooming back down the motorways towards Minsmere.

David Tomlinson tells me that he never once broke the speed limit, but the 250 miles from Bempton to Minsmere, between Tree Sparrow at 00.22 a.m. and Spotted Crake at 04.03 were covered in 3 hours 41 minutes, an average speed of 69.44 m.p.h. So I guess we have to believe him.

Back at Blythburgh for a super sausage, egg, bacon, beans fry-up provided by our stalwart band of helpers, Mr McGill duly appeared and chatted away with his notebook for the 35 minute break we then enjoyed. Mr McGill said he would like to meet up with us again and see what birdwatching was really like and we made an appointment to meet him at the Lowestoft Coastguards. That was the last we saw of him. But Angus, brilliant journalist he is, turned this adversity to advantage and produced an exceptionally amusing centre spread in the *Evening Standard* the following Wednesday. Evidently he had duly found the Lowestoft Coastguards, but not believing that birdwatchers would seriously head for an area dominated by Gas Works, rubbish tips and decaying factories, had moved on elsewhere in search of more likely-looking bird habitats. A few gems from his piece will give the feel of his day.

The *ffPS* team in 1981 : *left to right* Bill Oddie, Cliff Waller, Tim Inskipp and John Gooders (*Photo Angus McGill*)

'I joined Bill Oddie's lot for breakfast at 11.00 a.m., a civilised hour. As a strictly impartial observer I was on their side from that moment.'

'I got to Lowestoft all right and I found the sea-wall. It was right there by the sea.'

'But wait, what was sitting on that pile sticking out of the sea? A *bird*, a very depressed-looking bird, a seagull, no less. Very rare in some parts, I shouldn't wonder. And there was another and another. Every pile had a gull on it. This intelligence, I felt, must be passed on to Mr Oddie at once.'

'They had been very busy said the coastguards. They had got the pair of Black Redstarts at the Gas-works, and the Eiders beside the pier, the Iceland Gull that had been there all winter and the Kitti-wakes on the roof of the old Pavilion. There used to be summer shows in the Pavilion and sometimes you couldn't hear the actors for the Kittiwakes on the roof'.

We met up with Angus McGill again the following day at Huntingfield where we all listened in rapt atten-tion to the adventures that had befallen him along the coast at Lowestoft. It put our exploits truly into the shade. Each year Angus wishes us luck, but it will, I fear, be a long, long time before he sets foot along that treacherous coast again.

Angus was right, we did do well at Lowestoft with a complete wipe-out of the species we expected to see, aided by our man on the spot, 'Big' Brian. *Country Life* dipped out on Black Redstart, Iceland Gull, Purple Sandpiper and Eider, which was bad enough. How-ever, their pain was doubled when the BBC crew told them that they had just filmed the Black Redstart singing atop the Gas Works. This really was a duff period for the *Country Life* lot. By 11.30 they were on 129. Two hours later they were still on the same score, while we had in the meantime broken the record and were on 135. By 14.30 we were up to 137 with a sur-prising Buzzard, the hoped-for Golden Plover and were 4 ahead. By 15.16 we had gone one more ahead follow-ing a search for a Little Owl with the aid of some good gen and an out-of-date Ordnance Survey map.

After going up and down a village High Street that shall be nameless at least half a dozen times we dis-covered that the pub we were looking for had been

To dip out on: to fail to see/hear an expected bird.

delicensed and converted to a private house. Only then did the other landmarks fall into place and we spotted the owl watching us from atop the appropriate barn. Doubtless he had seen it all, but had not even had the courtesy to call. So there we were at 16.16 on 138 and still 3 birds ahead – a fact we found out only later when we met up with the television crew at Cley. Thereafter things fell apart and what could have been a triumph ended as a total disaster.

We were beaten by three clear species, 143 to 146. A total of 157 species was seen in all and over £3,000 was raised for distribution between bird charities.

Sir Peter Scott had very generously offered us one of his paintings as a prize to be held by the winners for a year. However, we thought that something quite silly would really be more appropriate and so it was that an addled Néné Goose's egg, signed by Sir Peter, was presented to the victorious much travelled players, while the handsome gentlemen of the *ffPS* choked back their emotion and accepted defeat with a stiff upper lip.

The participants in the '*Country Life* Record Birdwatch' have always been conscious of the problems involved in watching rare birds susceptible to disturbance, and the teams have adhered strictly to the rules formulated by David Tomlinson. As a result three separate species were placed 'out of bounds' in 1982. The Cranes that had recently summered 'somewhere in East Anglia' were not to be disturbed by either team. The colony of Golden Orioles, which by 1981 had grown to 12 or 14 pairs in Suffolk, was not to be visited. And Red-backed Shrikes, now down to less than 20 pairs in Suffolk, were not to be sought at their known breeding grounds. (By sheer good fortune a migrant shrike appeared at Weybourne to the delight of the *ffPS*, but to the chagrin of *Country Life* who missed it.) So three species were deliberately ruled out by the two teams in 1982. The same birds were ruled out in 1983 and will be in future unless circumstances change.

Within weeks of the 'Big Bird Race '81' being over we were deep into negotiations with a company called Dragon that wanted to make a 50 minute film for the then unborn Channel 4 television. We, and especially Bill, had very strong ideas about the sort of film we wanted to see and by sheer good fortune Major Steadman of Dragon Films had the same ones.

The addled Néné's egg and its magnificent container, a Victorian eggwarmer discovered by John Burton in a Suffolk sale (*Photo David Tomlinson*)

Each team would be followed throughout the day by its own crew and director. Though we would give interviews and talk to camera, the film was to be a documentary reporting what actually happened rather than getting us to pretend to be birdwatching on the day before or after the event. Yours truly was appointed to see to the finances and ensure that Dragon made a significant contribution to the bird charities we were supporting; and soon a deal was struck.

Though still called the '*Country Life* Record Bird-watch', 1982's event was inevitably to become 'The Great Bird Race'. We were deprived of the services of Tim Inskipp who was away in Nepal studying the future of the Great Indian Bustard and the Bengal Florican. In books we would now have cast high and wide in our search for a replacement. In fact we all settled straight away on Ron Johns. Ron has seen more birds in Britain than anyone else and was my companion on an expedition to Morocco for a month way back in 1970. He was an obvious choice and one of the very few field observers who could adequately replace Tim.

Meanwhile we had agreed with David Tomlinson to a change in the Rules. In future both teams would start and finish at the same spot, thus providing the media with every opportunity to film the event.

The whole point of the exercise is to raise money, and by making a more filmable event we hoped to generate even more interest from the media, and thus more sponsors.

David also thought that the time wasted in a mad dash from Yorkshire to Suffolk could have been better spent. And so it was agreed. Both teams would finish at Blythburgh as the previous year. But rather than get up and start together, we reached an amicable com-promise: both teams would have to be within 20 miles of Saxmundham at midnight. We were . . . fast asleep. *Country Life* were . . . ticking off Nightingale in our own backyard at Blythburgh at 00.01.

Having decided on a slightly later start we awoke at 03.00 to find ourselves 18 species behind. At our own personal Long-eared Owl spot we were surprised to find a Mercedes G-wagen and another group of would-be owl spotters equipped with walkie-talkies. This turned out to be *Country Life*'s back-up team! Back-up team? Walkie-talkies? What would they think of next?

By 06.22 *Country Life* reached the 100 mark and won the special prize for doing so. Barbour had donated a Mallard sculpture by Val Bennett and a cheque for £100 to the county naturalists' trust where the 100th bird was recorded. At this point we were 25 birds behind and had very little out of the ordinary to compensate. We then went on one of those little walkabouts that our team seems so prone to and wasted 45 minutes searching for Willow Tit. We breakfasted at 10.30 having taken in Minsmere and made a few gains on the opposition's home ground.

The 150 barrier was broken for the first time by *Country Life* at Weybourne at 19.20 with a late Golden Plover. Meanwhile we were still on 144, six birds behind. Mopping up in North Norfolk took its time and it was dark before we gave up on the Golden Plover with Bill and Ron having heard the bird while Cliff and I were exploring the other end of the damp field it inhabited. It seemed then that we could not possibly make it. We had left Titchwell at the same time, but were now two hours behind. So we drove southwards watching the fuel gauge on our eye-catching six-wheel Range Rover lent by Pace Petroleum and decorated in their red, white and blue racing colours.

For the *Country Life* team the last few hours of the event were spent motoring back to Suffolk via the Brecks where at 22.46 they eventually heard a Stone Curlew. With less than an hour and a quarter to get across the finishing line they had certainly cut it fine. We meanwhile made our last desperate effort to locate a Little Owl, failed and finished at 23.55. *Country Life* finished at '24.09' – their total 152 to our 151.

At the end of a long hard day, preceded by a short night's sleep, tempers tend to get a bit frayed and there were some harsh words said about winning by a single bird and then being late to finish. I suppose that David Tomlinson could have been magnanimous and called it a draw, but that is not David. He was jubilant at winning and I suppose we would have been as well. The trouble is that I could not help remembering what David had said to me the previous day. 'We aren't going to worry about being a few minutes late are we?' I agreed that we were not. Surely he hadn't banked on Stone Curlew at 22.46 p.m.? Or had he?

We sat numbed by having come so close to success

Stone Curlew

27

and debated a change in the Rules once more to cover lateness. A penalty seemed appropriate, but not disqualification. Personally I do not think we deserved to win – we had made too many mistakes. But the '*Country Life* Record Birdwatch' came very close to disaster that evening and the following day.

The whole event had been filmed by Dragon throughout the day and a total of nearly £5,000 had been raised. It had been a good effort and with growing interest the future of the event looked settled. Clearly the more media coverage we got the more support we could hope to attract.

A week before the 1983 'off' the *ffPS* crew were busily wriggling away at the Bird Race Disco courtesy of the Natural History Museum in London's Cromwell Road. Cyril Walker and his team of helpers (willing and otherwise) made a tremendous success of the event with rousing and quite deafening music preventing any potential eavesdropping or bugging by the opposition. Thus an ornitho-Watergate affair was happily avoided. Bill spent most of the evening handing out prizes and helping people part with their money, while Cyril had sub-contracted his role as chief organiser to Bob Ivison, though retaining the function of Chief Bouncer – an essential at any successful disco he informed me.

The disco gave us the opportunity to get right up to date with our preparations and Cyril took time off from throwing impecunious gate-crashing twitchers from the Museum steps to escort us through the elaborate plans that had been laid. Mark Carwardine had organised a back-up team of immense proportions. There would, we were informed, be individuals and small groups scattered across East Anglia locating scarce and difficult birds for us and (presumably) hiding them from the *Country Life* team by dint of sheer numbers. The whole organisation would liaise through the telephone system and the team must 'phone in to base, as they had promised in previous years, but had singularly failed to do. Bill and I were impressed and vowed by Elton John (some sort of pop deity, I gather) that we would.

And so it was that we gathered once more at Cliff Waller's Suffolk cottage on the inauspicious Friday the thirteenth of May ready for the midnight 'off'. Bill, Tim, Cliff and myself had an hour or so of gentlemanly

planning and debate of the starting hour. Would we lose our image if we started at midnight? And what was hidden behind the *Country Life* team's request to change the starting distance to 35 miles, not 20 miles, of Saxmundham? Could we break the 150 species barrier again and was 160 humanly possible? The 'phone rang virtually constantly as the *ffPS* grapevine reported rare, and not so rare, birds from all over East Anglia.

We could do no more. Only the next 24 hours or so would prove whether all the effort and teamwork would produce the result we desired.

Alarm bells rang and bleary-eyed we gathered in the kitchen for coffee/tea/toast (delete as necessary) and we were (as they say in books) ready for the fray. But that is another story . . . what happened you can read about exclusively only in the pages that follow.

The *ffPS* team's 1983 planning session in Angel Cottage: *left to right* Bill Oddie, the back of Cliff Waller, Tim Parmenter, Tim Inskipp, John Gooders and the standing Cyril Walker (*Photo B. R. Ivison*)

David Tomlinson
(*Photo Janet Tomlinson*)

Peter Smith
(*Photo David Tomlinson*)

THE *COUNTRY LIFE* TEAM

Jeremy Sorensen
(*Photo David Tomlinson*)

Bill Urwin
(*Photo David Tomlinson*)

The Account of the Country Life team

DAVID TOMLINSON

IT's A STRANGE THING, TIME. It goes as fast as a
Needle-tailed Swift flying with the wind, and like the
wind, you cannot see it. See it or not, you know that it
is passing, and it is quite amazing how fast it passes
during a 24-hour birdwatch, or twitch if you really
want to call it that. At midnight the whole day stretches
in front of you, and those first few hours pass slowly,
gaining momentum steadily, though by 08.00, with
well over a hundred species safely under your belt (or
to be more exact, down on the list), you still feel you
have as much time as you can possibly need. By noon,
or half-time, the rate of scoring has declined to such an
extent that you suddenly realise that those 12 remaining
hours are not going to be enough to see all the birds you
want to see, to visit all the habitats you should.

If only you could squeeze a few extra hours into a
day, just think how many more birds you could find!
So far I have only come up with one idea as to how it
can be done: spend the morning birding in Suffolk,
notch up 130 species or so, then jump on Concorde
and nip across the Atlantic. You would reach New
York at the same time as you left home, and within
minutes you could be looking for grackles, American
Robins and Chimney Swifts. The trouble is that
poor old British Airways is trying so hard to make
a profit that it isn't very likely to give the *Country Life*
team a free ride on Concorde.

The dream of Concorde first occurred to me as I sat
musing by the swimming pool of Taita Game Lodge,
in southern Kenya. The date was 30th November, and
though the gentle fluting of the African orioles in the
palms and the flapping of millions of butterfly wings

Gannet

was having a soporific effect on me, my mind was sufficiently alert to work out that there were exactly 180 days to go to the THE day, 14th May, the day of the fourth *Country Life* Record Birdwatch.

At the time my plans for the day were already forming. Concorde may have been a day dream, but I was quite prepared to settle for a helicopter. Staying one jump ahead of the *ffPS* mob is far from easy, but if we could jump in a chopper, then victory was sure to be ours. Combined with our Porsche, and of course the G-wagen, and who could touch us?

So I set my heart on a helicopter, and when I got back to England, I swung into action, writing to the US Air Force (one of their East Anglian bases is a good site for Woodlarks) asking them if they had a spare chopper, and perhaps a pilot, for the day. I even hinted I would give them a ride in the Porsche in return, as Americans love fast cars, even if they are not allowed to drive at much more than a canter. It was obvious to me that the US Air Force would be delighted to ferry my team around East Anglia, and might even take us up to Bempton to see the Gannets again. (Now what would Bill Oddie or Cliff Waller say to that?) The possibilities seemed endless, while just think what excellent public relations it would be for the Americans!

If by chance you are reading this, Colonel Gilbert, commanding officer of the 6th Air Calvary, USAF, I hope you are feeling guilty, for I do think you could have had the decency to reply to my letter.

However, if one can't fly in the sky, the next best thing is to fly along the roads, so I duly opted to use a Porsche for transport once again. My hardest decision is choosing the right Porsche: last year I turned down a 911 Turbo due to lack of space, but fortunately Porsche came to our rescue with the 911 Cabriolet, which being a convertible gives unlimited headroom. This is a very valuable asset when birdwatching, though it does have its disadvantages – if it rains.

A 911 may be a tough and rugged sports car, and its pedigree may include winning the Monte Carlo rally, but there are places where one should not really take £24,000-worth of high-performance machinery. The answer to this little problem is simple: back it up with the world's fastest four-wheel-drive cross-country vehicle, a Mercedes G-wagen. So this year, for the second consecutive year, our back-up team travelled in style in the G, as it soon became known, helping us out whenever we needed off-road transport, such as along the beach at Minsmere.

So with the vehicles decided upon, the next decision was to be who would be travelling in them. Here there was no need for any change, for as many football managers have learnt to their cost, you should never change a winning combination. Jeremy Sorensen, warden of Minsmere, the RSPB's showpiece reserve, has been an essential member of the team from the beginning. Jeremy modestly claims to have seen fewer birds in Britain than anyone else who has been birdwatching as long as he has. Well, he may not have seen them, but I am sure he has heard them, for he has a pair of ears that are second to none. He doesn't just identify birds by their song, but I swear he can tell them by the way they suck in air between notes. Add this ability to his inexhaustable energy (a former colleague of his once complained to me that the trouble with Jeremy was that he did everything at a run) and his intimate knowledge of Minsmere and you can see why he is such an important member of the team.

Peter Smith, like Jeremy, is not very big (they both just fit in the back of the Porsche), and he too is a man with great reserves of energy. Peter is the only Suffolk man in the team, and though he now lives in Sussex, surrounded by his own 7-acre oak wood (the best place to see roding Woodcock that I know) complete with trout stream, Grey Wagtails and Kingfishers, he still has a strong affinity for his home county. Though he insists that the Bird Race is the only day's birdwatching he does every year, at least in Britain, this is far from the truth, as his ability in the field proves. A geophysicist by profession, his job has taken him to many distant places in search of oil, and he delights in telling of swimming in a desert pool with Red-necked Phalaropes for company. As John Gooders has explained in the introduction, it was Peter's 'Big Day' exploits with David Pearson back in the early '60s which first inspired me to start the '*Country Life* Record Birdwatch'.

David Pearson lives in Kenya, and though he was home on leave in May 1980 and thus took part in the first Birdwatch, he has not been available since. His place has been taken by Bill Urwin, schoolteacher, and

In this account of the
Country Life team's
progress, Bill Urwin
is usually referred to
as 'Bill Urwin',
rather than simply
as 'Bill'. This is an
attempt to avoid
confusion with Bill
Oddie, the author of
the rival account.
The publishers
extend their
apologies to Bill
Urwin for this
relentless formality,
which is in no way
intended to reflect
any lack of warmth
in his personality!

at 30 the youngest member of the team. Bill comes from somewhere up north (the sort of place where you might look for wintering White-billed Divers and Ross's Gulls), and his beard, woolly hat and extensive British list strongly hint at the fact that he is the only true twitcher in the *Country Life* team. Twitcher he may be, but he also finds time to warden the Norfolk Naturalists' Trust reserve of Upton Broad, not far from his home at Acle, to grow outstanding asparagus, and have a pretty good knowledge of, among other things, flowers and insects. He is even threatening to give up twitching next year in favour of flies. For Bill, the greatest frustration of the Bird Race is not being insured to drive the Porsche; but he bears the agony of sitting in the co-driver's seat very well, and it does mean his energy is saved for finding birds, which he is very good at.

Then there's me. I have been addicted to birds since I was about five (can't remember much before that), and have pursued my quarry around much of the world, ranging from Texas to the Transvaal, Thailand to Trinidad, which doesn't leave time for twitching in Britain. I am a fairly competitive person, at least on the tennis or squash court, so my approach to the Bird Race is one of setting out to win. I also admit to a passion for fast cars, so the Bird Race is a fusion of my enthusiasm for both cars and birds.

One of the keys to success of a big day is local knowledge, which is not so easy to come by if you live in Kent, as I do. This is where the back-up team proved so valuable in 1982, becoming vital members of the combined *Country Life* effort. This year Derek Moore again agreed to organise the back-up, leaving poor old Cliff (with whom Derek has done much birding), to be heard muttering that 'Derek's gone over to the other side . . .' If you gain Derek you also get support from Derek's army of friends in the Suffolk Ornithologists' Group (again, much to Cliff's anguish), a very useful asset. Derek has one other great advantage as a back-up man – he has an inexhaustible supply of birding stories that can cheer you up when all else is going wrong.

Derek has in turn recruited Steve Piotrowski to ride shotgun in the G-wagen. Steve is not, as far as I know, a member of Solidarity, nor can he speak Polish with a Suffolk accent, but he is an ace birder. It took him a little while to recover from the 1982 recce, when the

speed of the Porsche on the straight Fenland roads led
to a slight loss of colour, but he has adjusted to the
pace of the G-wagen.

I think it was Napoleon who said that an army mar-
ches on its stomach; if it wasn't it should have been.
There may not be enough of us to count as an army,
and we try to do as little marching as possible, but we
do seem to spend a lot of the day munching. This is all
thanks to my wife, Jan, who is responsible for feeding
us. Work starts on the menu weeks before, for we eat
nothing but the best, and the final run-up to the Bird
Race sees the Tomlinson kitchen a hive of activity as
the food – ranging from smoked salmon sandwiches to
fine fruit cakes – is prepared. It seems a shame to have
such a feast and not wash it down with a glass or two of
St-Emilion, or perhaps a chilled Chablis, but we content ourselves with fruit juices and water instead, as we
cannot risk the possibility of impairing our powers of
identification. (Even more important, it might send us
to sleep, something else we have to go without during
the Bird Race).

With the Bird Race still months away, the hardest
chore begins: recruiting sponsors. The *ffPS* team have
wisely delegated this chore to Cyril Walker; I do the
Country Life fund raising. Once or twice a week Cyril and
I compare notes, to check on progress, and also ensure
that we don't both ask the same company. A time of
recession is not ideal for attempting to part a company
from its money, but I think we can be pleased with our
success. Many of the *Country Life*'s team sponsors have
backed us for three or even four years, and we are
particularly grateful to them for their continuing support.

Sponsors are usually invited to back us at the rate of
£1 per species recorded, giving another good reason
for finding the maximum possible number of birds in
the day. However, as all athletes know, there comes a
time when it becomes increasingly difficult to break
existing records, and we have now reached that point.
Good weather, the right wind and, of course, luck, all
start to play their part, but where possible we try and
ensure that our preparation leaves nothing missing.
From December onwards I send regular newsletters to
my team, and the first full meeting, or council of war,
is in April.

Our planning meeting this year was on 16th April, an idyllic day of blue skies and unbroken sunshine. We held the meeting in Jeremy's garden at Minsmere, with freshly arrived Swallows twittering overhead, Chiff-chaffs and Willow Warblers everywhere, and the odd burst of song from a Nightingale which clearly thought summer had arrived. (It hadn't, needless to say: it poured all the next day). All members of the team were present and correct, and with the help of a fine buffet prepared by Jan, and several glasses of Italian plonk, we got down to business.

Where, and when, should we start? In 1982, until the very last minute (or, to be honest, until about eight hours before midnight) we had planned to run our route in reverse, starting in the Brecks and finishing at Minsmere. Our practice run, following this route the weekend before, had proved satisfactory, and we had recorded just over 140 species, but it was something of a gamble, and we decided to play safe and start, as usual, at Minsmere, or at least in the Minsmere vicinity. The trouble is that there are several birds which require a special journey to be certain of seeing them: the only way to be sure of finding a Stone Curlew, for example, is a trip to the Brecks. Should we go there at midnight, then come back to Minsmere for dawn?

Questions like this continued to be debated, in between more good stories about birding on the Scillies, contributed by Derek, until a formula or plan of some kind was worked out. Barn Owls have always eluded us (though in 1981 we saw two on the drive back to Minsmere from the finish at Walberswick), and Bill Urwin thought he had a good site near to his home. If we started there at midnight, we could tick off Barn Owl, then drive by way of Lowestoft to take in Kitti-wake, which nest on the pier and on buildings close by. We could thus get another bird out of the way without having to return to Lowestoft again in the morning traffic.

For the last two years the *ffPS* team have stayed in bed until 03.00 or so, while we have chased around throughout the night. Would they be stung by their narrow defeat last year into following our example? We would certainly be kicking off at the stroke of midnight, for every second is precious. Though we provisionally arranged much of our route, we left it sufficiently flexible to allow for last minute changes, while we agreed on a practice run the Saturday before to check on times and distances. In 1982 we had lost a lot of time by not always knowing exactly where we were going, or taking a wrong turn, or even making a time-consuming diversion to west Norfolk to take in a reserve where we found nothing new. Cut out all the time wasting and we would have another two or even three hours to play with, and as I have said before, time is the most precious commodity.

There is an old saying that practice makes perfect, so

The approximate final route of the *Country Life* team (based on an Oxford University Press map)

on 7th May, with just a week to go, Bill Urwin, Derek, Steve and I practised the route we had decided on. The aim of the day wasn't so much to see birds as to work out times, distances and exactly how long each move would take. We used a Ford Sierra 2.3 for the recce, working on the principle that any time we managed in the Sierra we would beat in the Porsche, though the Sierra handled and went so well that really there was unlikely to be much real difference. The Porsche's great advantage is its ability to overtake and make the most of short gaps with such ease, but I have to admit (albeit reluctantly) that a Sierra is a much more comfortable way for four grown men to go birdwatching than a 911 Cabriolet, but the latter is a hell of a lot more fun.

We only recorded 127 birds on the recce, a figure which did not worry us at all. Far more important, we had proved that we could leave Minsmere at 08.30, take in several sites in the south of Suffolk, even as far away as Alton Water, reach North Norfolk by lunchtime, and be back in Suffolk by 18.00. Furthermore, after much debating the pros and cons of heading north or south from Minsmere, we finally decided that we would go south from Minsmere, even if it meant throwing away a useful time advantage over the other team. Knowing our estimated time of arrival at each site is also of great value to our various helpers dotted around the Suffolk countryside, all organised with great skill by Derek.

Only one real worry was left: the weather. Bad weather could ruin the day, and the cold, wet and windy days preceding 14th May did not leave room for any optimism. Our route was chosen, our supporting team was ready and waiting; but torrential rain could ruin everything, and leave us looking very wet and miserable in our convertible Porsche. There was nothing we could do except sit back and wait, as the countdown to 14th May began. Only time would tell what the weather would do to us, and that time was slipping away . . .

Five minutes to midnight . . . I checked my watch for the sixth time in as many minutes, waiting impatiently for the off. Those last few dying seconds of Friday 13th May, dragged on, leaving the *Country Life* team waiting impatiently for the stroke of midnight, the moment of truth. Of course it wasn't really the moment of truth, as there were 86,640 seconds, or 1,460 minutes, or 24 hours of truth to come, but it was midnight we were waiting for. We were standing in a line on a muddy footpath fringing a Broadland reedbed, just within the 20-mile radius of Lowestoft, listening for a Savi's Warbler to sing. Now Savi's Warbler is one of Britain's rarest breeding birds, and has a distinctive, far-carrying reeling song, not unlike the much commoner Grasshopper Warbler, but with a very different pitch. Last year we had heard a Savi's Warbler singing at Walberswick, and though we knew that a Savi's had been heard singing there again this year, our chances of hearing it did not seem high. So instead we headed north to this forlorn spot in the Norfolk Broads, where Bill had heard two singing Savi's only 48 hours before.

Flower twitching must be very dull, for flowers cannot fly away, but there are times when I wish that birds couldn't fly. In the car, on the way north, Bill Urwin had insisted that hearing the Savi's 'would be no trouble. They were going so well on Wednesday you could even hear 'em from the road.' Needless to say, not even a peep was forthcoming from the Savi's Warblers as the clock ticked away to midnight. Of course, it might have been even more frustrating if the wretched birds had started singing at 23.45, then gone silent shortly before midnight, but at least it would have given us a chance to tune our ears to their song, for it was almost exactly a year since I had last listened to one.

Savi's Warblers or no Savi's Warblers, the stroke of midnight did mean that the 'Big Bird Race' was officially under way. Fifteen minutes earlier the local Tawny Owls had been making such a din that you could almost think they had just been told a good joke and wanted to tell everyone in the neighbourhood; but by midnight they had gone silent. It fell to a Sedge Warbler, chuntering away at his song only a few feet from us, to open the batting with a quick single. Time 00.00½. Sedge Warbler. We were off! Like hitting the first ball in an important squash match, the action of noting the first bird had a relaxing effect on the team: at long last we could start looking at birds, or rather listening for them, rather than constantly

Sedge Warbler

peering at watch faces ticking off the minutes.

We had a quick flurry of activity as birds called around us: the Sedge was joined by a reeling Grasshopper Warbler, reminding me of the problems the *ffPS* team had had finding a 'Gropper' last year, while we had heard our first within yards of Cliff's cottage. (Very satisfying that, though it would have been even better if they had known at the time that we had poached a Gropper off their own patch.) In 1982 Grasshopper Warbler was our third bird of the day, this year it had pulled up into second place, taking over from Black-headed Gull, which now dropped to third.

The day was not yet two minutes old when a Moorhen called away to our right, and seconds later the Tawny Owls started again, their disconsolate hoots floating easily on the still night air. The fact that the air was still was quite remarkable, for the previous day had been windy – far from ideal conditions for listening for birds. I glanced skywards, and could just make out a few stars, though a thin layer of cloud was doing its best to shroud them from view. The weather forecast was far from good, and as it had rained for every one of the previous 28 days, there seemed no good reason to expect 14th May to be dry.

There was now a seven minute gap before our next addition to the list was noted, seven minutes of straining ears listening for the Savi's, and seven minutes of wondering whether I was really wise to enjoy a lunch of champagne and stuffed crab with one of my sponsors less than 10 hours before. I tried resting my eyes by shutting them, but for some curious reason found my ears work best when my eyes are open. Surely I wasn't feeling tired already?

A distant piping from across the marsh woke me up with a start, and Jeremy (who always does a splendid job of keeping our score) jotted down Oystercatcher in the sixth slot on the score sheet. Oystercatchers are noisy birds, and had been our fifth bird of the day in 1982. It was while Jeremy was scribbling down Oystercatcher, his torch clamped between his teeth, that I first heard what I thought was a Savi's. Bill Urwin had heard it too, but it was too brief for us to be sure, especially as the Sedge Warbler bashing away in front of us had already proved what a splendid mimic he was.

At sixteen minutes past midnight there was a short

but distinctive squeal from a Water Rail, a pleasing bird to get so early in the day, and one we had not found last year. We were still congratulating ourselves on this piece of luck when at long last the Savi's decided that he had teased us for quite long enough, and gave a brief burst of unmistakable song. Success! Delighted that our gamble had proved so worthwhile, we trudged back through the mud to the car, Jeremy's Volvo 360GLS. Using the Volvo wasn't a cunning move by us to slip unnoticed past Cliff's cottage at 23.00; we had decided not to use the Porsche until we left Minsmere, as we intended to keep the hood down, come what may, but thought it could be somewhat cold topless at midnight. So for the first time ever on a Bird Race, Bill and I travelled on the back seat while Jeremy threaded his way through the lanes and down to Breydon Water.

We weren't the only birdwatchers afoot at midnight. Derek had left Jeremy's bungalow at the same time as us – 22.45 – and picked up another of our helpers, Reg Clarke, from the regular Minsmere watering hole, the Eel's Foot, and the two of them had headed north in our bright red G-wagen, well covered with our sponsors stickers, to South Cove, where a Corncrake was rumoured to be singing every night.

Now Corncrake is one species that Derek hasn't got on his Suffolk list (which stands, at the time of writing, at 263), so he was particularly keen to try and hear this bird. Alas, all they managed to record was a distant Little Owl, the clicking of the G-wagen's clock, and not much else. So back they headed for Minsmere's Meadow Marsh to try for a possible Spotted Crake. Jeremy had warned them that no Spotted Crakes had been spotted, or even heard, in Meadow Marsh for something like 30 years, but it is such splendid crake habitat there really ought to be one there. (Any Spotted Crakes reading this might like to go along next year and give it a try.) Needless to say, there wasn't, though the crake hunters were a little taken back when they thought they saw the approaching lights of another vehicle. Could Cliff have sent out spies to follow the G-wagen? It turned out to be the distant lights of Sizewell Power Station. You might well ask how I could employ a back-up team who have difficulty in telling a power station from a car, but I can assure you that they are much better on birds.

Savi's Warbler

Last year we had recorded a Long-eared Owl during the Bird Race, and we were keen to try and do the same again this year, especially as we felt sure that Cliff would have a Long-eared Owl site sorted out for his team. So Derek's next chore was to check out a couple of Long-eared Owl sites. Unfortunately, it wasn't really Derek's night, and once again he drew a blank, not even hearing a hint of a hoot. Spirits were now low in the G, and the previous night's optimism had evaporated. Later Derek's most interesting sighting was a brief glimpse of Cliff's battered Land Rover, the vehicle the enemy (is it too rude to call them that?) traditionally use in the early hours of the morning. It was evident that the *ffPS* were taking this year's challenge more seriously, and were not slumbering on in their previous fashion. We never did find our Long-eared Owl, though of course *ffPS* did. Perhaps we should have posted a few spies to follow the Land Rover and see where it went . . .

By now the intrepid quartet of Jeremy, Bill Urwin, Peter and I had arrived at Breydon Water, picking our way through the old station yard to the sea wall. A quick scramble up, and we were rewarded with the Desert Island Disc sound of a Herring Gull – bird no. 9. Much more pleasing, both to the ear and the score sheet, was the beautiful cry of a Curlew we heard a minute later, for Curlew was one bird we were not confident of seeing later in the day. (As it turned out we did see one at Titchwell in the late afternoon. To be honest it could have even been a Whimbrel, but as by this time we needed neither for the list, I did not waste the energy to raise my binoculars to my eyes.)

10 species

Breydon Water at high tide is an excellent area for waders, and if only we had been able to see out across the estuary we would certainly have picked up several more species. As it was we had to be content with a distant *craakk* from a passing Grey Heron, the laughing quack of a Shelduck, and the piping of a Ringed Plover. Back into the Volvo we climbed, one hour into the day, and with 13 species recorded, three more than at the same stage last year. We pottered a few hundred yards into Yarmouth, and tried listening for singing Black Redstarts, though why on earth a Black Redstart should be singing at 01.00 in the morning I have no idea. We weren't too disappointed not to hear one, so

Time 01.00

we got back in the car and headed south to Lowestoft, another famous Black Redstart site.

Country Life

DAVID TOMLINSON

In hindsight it is perhaps remarkable that four men in green Barbour jackets, carrying torches and binoculars and prowling around the Bird's Eye factory at 01.30 on a Saturday morning, were not apprehended by the local constabulary. No doubt we would have been if the local constabulary had spotted us, but they didn't, and nor did we spot a Black Redstart. (Rumour has it that the GLC has ruled that all Black Redstarts living in London must now be called by their scientific name, *Phoenicurus ochruros*, until a new name is devised which does not use the word black.)

Once again we weren't really surprised not to find any Black Redstarts up and about at such an early hour, but we did shine the headlights of the car down one of the waterbreaks in the hope of spotting a roosting Purple Sandpiper. No luck, so we wandered over to the harbour to look for diving ducks and grebes in the lights of the port. The security man on the gate looked at us suspiciously, so we shouted to him that we were only looking for birds, which seemed to satisfy him, as he must have encountered mad birders before, though not, I should think, so early in the morning. There were a few gulls on the water, and Peter gave a sudden shout when he spotted a pair of duck. They proved to be Mallard, our first new bird for 40 minutes.

Our real reason for visiting Lowestoft wasn't to try and find Black Redstarts, nor was it our only reliable site for Mallard. It was to tick off the Kittiwakes which nest on the pier. So down the pier we trundled, past a couple of bobbies in a panda car who looked at us in a bemused sort of way, but clearly thought we were not worth wasting time on, and over several sleeping policemen (those horrible bumps they put in roads to make you slow down). Having bumped our way over several of these we reached the Kittiwake cliff, or the nearest thing to a Kittiwake cliff in Suffolk. Sure enough, there they were, and not only did we see them, but we also heard the odd cry of *kittiwake*. Very obliging birds.

Kittiwake

A quick check out to sea revealed nothing more exciting than a Lesser Black-backed Gull, but down on the list it went, one bird less to look for as the day wore on.

Now it was time to check on the South Cove Corn-

Time 02.00

crake. If Derek had found it, he was to leave a note in the bus shelter at Wrentham on the nearby A12. Bill Urwin checked out the bus shelter with care, but there was no note for us, so we drove to the church at South Cove where the Corncrake was reputed to be calling. Straining our ears for the '*crex-crex*' of *Crex crex* (does any bird have a better scientific name?), we didn't even do as well as Derek, as no Little Owl broke the silence, and even the Volvo's clock proved inaudible. The Corncrake would have been a real bonus, but perhaps 14th May was not to be a bonus day. So down the road towards Southwold we drove, to the spot where the Saturday before we had seen a Barn Owl. Usual routine: stop the car, climb out, listen. Yes – what's that? No, nothing as exciting as a Barn Owl, but another Sedge Warbler, and slightly further away, a Reed Warbler, bird no. 17.

Our next halt was overlooking the Blyth estuary, and no sooner had we stopped the car than the 18th bird of the day was duly noted, a Nightingale, singing so well it almost sounded indignant that we had taken so long to hear it. In previous years the Nightingale has always been our first bird of the day, while this year it had slumped to a lowly 18th place. However, this was not a reflection of a sudden scarcity of Nightingales in Suffolk – far from it, for 1983 has proved to be a bumper year for the Nightingale, with Minsmere boasting some 60 or so singing males, a 300% increase since the mid '70s.

For the next few hours we were rarely to be out of earshot of Nightingales, but it was at Blythburgh that we heard another welcome sound, the unmistakable whistling call of the Whimbrel, which earns the bird its old country name of seven-whistler. Had Cliff and his team heard the same bird? From the lay-by where we had parked at the side of the A12 we could see Cliff's cottage, but there was not a glimmer of light, leaving us to debate whether they had already left, or whether they were still snoozing. We drove slowly past the cottage, but it was too dark to see whether Cliff's Land Rover was there, and it was not until a few minutes later, when we met up with Derek and the G-wagen, that we discovered that they were indeed out and about.

We found the G-wagen illuminated in our headlights as we drove back to Minsmere past the old saw mills.

Whimbrel

Derek and Reg were in low spirits, having found nothing of note, though they had seen a Barn Owl two minutes before. We had spent the previous 15 minutes trying to whistle up a Stone Curlew, with Bill Urwin doing his very best Stone Curlew calls, all to no avail. We were quite convinced that there were no Stone Curlews on this part of the Suffolk coast, and we still wonder whether the Stone Curlew recorded by the *ffPS* team was not, in fact, young Urwin pretending that he was a Stone Curlew. It is easy to be fooled when straining every square millimetre of your ear drum to try and hear what you want to hear, and though Bill Urwin may not be able to fool a Stone Curlew, his whistle is quite convincing. So perhaps we inadvertently boosted the *ffPS* score by one; we will never know.

By this time we had also survived three minor crises. The first was when I managed to lose the pencil, with which we were keeping the score, shortly after jotting down Lesser Black-backed Gull. Try as I would I couldn't find the thing, so we all ended up searching our pockets for some kind of writing implement. Peter quietly reminded me that he had suggested to Jeremy that perhaps we should take a spare pencil. Jeremy had replied that there was no need to, as he had his pen knife with him. After much rummaging a pen was at last unearthed, so we could keep the score once more.

The second crisis was of rather more minor nature, though it was a matter of life and death. Anyone who regularly drives between 02.00 and 03.00 will know that this is the hour when the hedgehog prowls, and in the course of half a dozen miles we narrowly missed running over three, the third and last having a particularly lucky escape as Jeremy jinked the Volvo round it at the last moment. You can buy rather nice stickers from the Fauna and Flora Preservation Society's HQ at London Zoo asking you not to squash hedgehogs, so it would have been very bad form to have left one of our prickly friends flattened in the road as evidence of our passing.

Crisis number three had rather more sinister overtones. Last year the *ffPS* team had failed to see a Little Owl, so they were bound to be trying very hard to make sure they got one this year. On the road past the saw mills there is an old ash tree which contains a Little Owl's nest, and we felt fairly sure that Cliff knew all about it. So when we saw a car parked a mere dozen feet from the nest tree, we automatically suspected enemy spies of staking the tree out. We drove closer – yes, the car was occupied. We shone our torch into it, expecting to find enemy back-up, carefully watching the nest hole. I will draw a delicate veil over what the torch revealed, but it is sufficient to say that the occupants of the car had other things on their mind than Little Owls.

It was time now to leave the Volvo, climb into the G-wagen and go off in search of the elusive Long-eared Owl. In Derek's skilful hands the G made light work of the heavy going as we bounced our way towards the owl site. By now the first few drops of rain were splattering the windscreen, dampening the ground and our enthusiasm. We climbed out of the vehicle and listened. And listened. And listened. No, however hard we tried, we couldn't turn the various nocturnal noises into the low hoot of the Long-eared Owl, but a distant honking of Canada Geese away on the marsh did give us our 20th bird at 02.56. This was soon followed by Woodpigeon at 03.06. We didn't actually see the pigeon, nor did we hear it coo (they don't do too much cooing at 3 a.m. on a wet May morning), but it burst out of its roost in a nearby larch with such gusto there was nothing else it could be. After a brief discussion we decided that we could count it.

It was shortly after this that Jeremy and Bill Urwin claimed to have heard a Nightjar churring in the distance. Peter thought that perhaps he could hear it, too, but I could hear nothing, and neither could Derek. After five minutes of struggling to try and hear this fabled bird whose existence I doubted, we all heard the distinctive flight note of a Nightjar close by – bird no. 23, joining Bittern, the distant boom of which we had heard six minutes before. It was quite a relief to get Nightjar out of the way, as this was one bird that could well prove very difficult to get if we did not hear it now. As it turned out it wouldn't have mattered, for later I saw a Nightjar hawking over one of the woodland rides in the grey light of dawn. Having given up on the Leo (Long-eared Owl), there was little the heath could offer us, so back in the G we went, and on down to the Scrape for a short interval before the dawn chorus got under way. By now the rain was falling steadily, and it was pretty chilly, too. At 03.40 a burst of explosive song

20 species
Time 03.00

Nightjar

from a Cetti's Warbler was a welcome sound, and one that Peter and David would hardly have been likely to recognise back on their early Big Days. There are several Cetti's at Minsmere now, and this was one bird we had no worries about recording.

A distant Cuckoo was shouting his name to the world as we stumbled in the dark and the rain towards the Scrape, tucking in to our first food of the day – brown rolls with rare beef. I can't say I am usually hungry at 03.45 in the morning, but when you have been up all night it's amazing how peckish you get. I was still stuffing down beef roll as we suddenly enjoyed a flurry of birds – in the space of a minute we added Avocet, Redshank, Skylark, Sandwich Tern, Lapwing and Coot to our tally, shortly followed by the nasal quack of a Gadwall, and a short trill of song from a Reed Bunting. Then, on the stroke of 4 a.m., a Spotted Redshank flew over, uttering its distinctive call three times. For a moment we forgot the rain, as Spotted Red was a good bird to record so early in the day, and one that we had missed in '82.

30 species

Time 04.00

There is no doubt that when dawn breaks, the best place to be at Minsmere is the wood, so at 04.04 we left the Scrape, and made our way back to the wood. It was still raining, but seemed to have eased off slightly. This is perhaps the most exciting part of the day, as new birds come more quickly than runs to Ian Botham, but I have to admit that it is not my favourite time. For some reason God gave me an excellent pair of eyes, but failed to match their performance to my ears. The net result is that I am tone deaf, which is quite a handicap when listening to bird song. However, as I have already mentioned, Jeremy has a pair of ears that seem to work as effectively as parabolic reflectors, and neither Bill nor Peter is exactly slow when it comes to picking up song. So I listen carefully, try very hard, and flatly refuse to be conned into hearing something my ear drums fail to register, much to the frustration of the rest of the team.

Having said all that, I might add that I am not *that* bad, and had no problems picking up the Robin, Redstart and Blackbird that were our next three birds, and heard the croak of a roding Woodcock as quickly as everyone else. The Woodcock was quite a bonus, as we had good views of it a couple of times as it flew past

A Woodcock rodes over the woodland at Minsmere. This ritual flight, accompanied by croaks and whistles, is a 'beating of the bounds' of the bird's territory.

40 species

us on slow-beating wings. This was about all we did see as we sheltered under a broad beech tree from a heavy downpour – what would we do if it rained all day? We stood and watched the rain pour down, and argued over the identity of a small bat hunting for midges round our tree. Pipistrelle or Daubenton's? I reckoned the former, Bill opted for the latter.

By now the dawn chorus was in full voice, with Cuckoos all around, and Tawny Owls having their last say before settling down for the day. New birds came thick and fast – Pheasant at 04.20, Song Thrush two minutes later, and then a Shoveler came flying over, readily identified by its silhouette. A burst of song to our right was a Wren, answered by another a few yards away, and the delightful warble of a cock Blackcap was our 43rd bird at 04.30. At this stage in 1982 we were only up to 32 species, so we were going well despite the weather.

Long-tailed Tits have a cheerful buzzing note I

never have any problems picking up, but such was the volume of bird song which surrounded us that I was quite unable to pick out this note among the surrounding din. Jeremy could hear it, so could Bill Urwin, so could Peter, but I couldn't, and nor was I going to be conned into thinking I had heard it. So Long-tailed Tit failed to go down on the list, but in the next nine minutes we did add Great Tit, Carrion Crow, Turtle Dove, Dunnock, Goldcrest, Chiffchaff and Blue Tit to reach 50 at 04.39. (In 1982 our 50th bird was Chaffinch at 05.08).

50 species

Part of the essential working equipment of Minsmere Bird Reserve are CB radios, and these we used to great effect on the Birdwatch. It was as we were walking through the wood, scoring fast and furiously, that we heard our first report of the enemies' back-up team. David Bakewell, who we had posted on Dunwich cliffs to look out for scoter, called us up on the CB to report that he was outnumbered four to one by *ffPS* back-up

Time 05.00

men, only to call us back moments later to report that they had driven off at great speed in a Saab. That was them all right. Somehow, knowing that the rival team was not far away, sharpened my step and woke me up, for I was still wondering about the wisdom of that champagne lunch, and feeling distinctly unlively.

False alarms are part of the day, and it was shortly after 05.00, with a further five species in the bag, bringing our total up to 55, that Jeremy thought he heard a Willow Tit. We scrambled through the damp woodland in the hope of getting closer, but if there was a Willow Tit, then it was keeping remarkably quiet. Jeremy thought he heard it again, so all ears aimed in the same direction. No luck. There were, Jeremy confirmed, a pair of Willow Tits present in this part of the wood, but they declined to call again, so this was one bird that we were doomed to miss altogether.

Certain birds are much later risers than others (just like some girls I have known), so as we walked back through the wood, retracing our steps exactly, we picked up a number of birds that had only just decided to add their voices to the dawn chorus. A Green Woodpecker yaffled away to one side, a call that reminded me of the old country name for the Green Woodpecker: the rain bird. Fortunately the rain had now stopped, though the sky looked a good deal less than happy.

However, I was feeling happier by now, for at long last there was enough light for me to start seeing things. No longer did I have to rely on my ears, but I could use my eyes as well. Jeremy paused for a Spotted Flycatcher he had just heard. I didn't hear it, but I could see it, and pointed it out to Bill Urwin and Peter. Overhead Starlings and Swifts were flying, a Great Spotted *60 species* Woodpecker was drumming close by, joined by a Lesser Spotted, an excellent bird to get out of the way, for the elusive Lesser Spotted Woodpecker can be a difficult bird to find.

At 05.32 we emerged from the wood, our list now boasting an impressive 66 species, soon to be joined by Mistle Thrush (our 130th species in 1982) and Yellowhammer. Walking down the track towards the Scrape once again and our CB crackled into life. David on the cliff reported he had scoters in sight, so the cliff was to be our next destination, a change of route from previous 50 years when we have visited Island Mere and then the

Scrape. It was this change of route that was to have a drastic effect on our scoring, slowing us down considerably.

Though it may have slowed us down, we still continued to pick up a steady stream of new species. A Teal flew low over the field behind Minsmere's reception hut, looking deceptively different in the poor light. I spotted House Sparrows feeding in a little cluster close to the reception hut, while our elevated position allowed us to look out over the Scrape, and spot a Mute Swan (or as they say in this part of Suffolk, 'a hooge moot swaan sitting on its nest'). Sand Martins were busy overhead, a charm of Goldfinches flew by, and I found a cock Wheatear in the field. It was really quite fun to start seeing birds rather than only hearing them, and I started to relax a little more and enjoy myself, shaking off the early morning blues.

70 species

If there is one area in which the *Country Life* team has much more talent than the *ffPS* mob it is athletic ability. With the lure of those scoters visible from the cliff, the entire team broke into a brisk jog down to the beach, passing Bearded Tit, Whitethroat and Jackdaw on the way. Once we reached the beach we all piled into the waiting G-wagen, which whisked us along to the foot of the cliff. Here we had another mad scramble, and for anyone who has never run up Dunwich cliff then I can assure you that it looks less steep than it really is. We arrived at the top panting as heavily as an overweight cocker spaniel which has just chased a young rabbit, and took a moment or two for us to get our breath back and concentrate on the job in hand. We took it in turns to look through David's 'scope and find the Common Scoter he had located a half a mile offshore. It was while waiting my turn at the 'scope that I found a Fulmar, our 80th species, but a minute later everyone had viewed the distant scoter, giving us a bird in the bag that we had never recorded before on a Bird Race day.

80 species

The scoter had lured us up on to the cliff, so to make the most of the position in which we found ourselves we had a quick look for Stonechat. The latter are really among the most helpful of birds, for they invariably sit on the very top of bushes in full view, while if you can't see one then they usually reveal their presence with their stone-chatting notes. This time we were in luck,

Time 06.00

See picture on
p. 126

and within minutes we had both heard and seen a Stonechat.

No time was to be wasted, so back down the cliff we went, scrambled into the G, and rushed along the beach back to the East Scrape hide. Here there was a real bonus bird sitting outside the hide – a splendid female Long-tailed Duck, another bird that we have never recorded before on a Birdwatch. This particular individual first arrived at Minsmere months before – I had seen it myself as long ago as February – and we all felt honoured that it had decided to stay at Minsmere long enough to be counted on the day. The previous week there had still been six Long-tails at Benacre, but these had now left, so it was a relief that the Minsmere Long-tail had not followed their example.

Waders are what the Scrape is famous for, and these were what we were looking for. Dunlin proved little problem, and Keith Fairclough, one of Minsmere's assistant wardens, had sorted out most of the birds we wanted to see. There was a good drake Wigeon grazing on island 55 (cunning idea giving all those little islands numbers. Trouble is I can never find the right number . . .). Suddenly I picked up a distant wader flying away from us. My mind raced – what was it? Almost instinctively I mouthed the words 'Green Sandpiper', and managed to direct everyone else in the same direction. Fortunately everyone did see it, though by the time Bill Urwin got on to it, it was little more than a distant speck. Was it really a Green Sand? he queried. Both Jeremy and I were 100% certain it was, but even so it was pleasing when our back-up team confirmed a few minutes later that they had flushed a Green Sandpiper by the sluice; it must have been the same bird I had spotted.

90 species

I was still congratulating myself on finding the Green Sand when Peter gave a shout for a Turnstone in splendid summer plumage, which flew past the hide and landed on one of the islands, and moments later he added a Black-tailed Godwit in glorious red plumage to his tally. This misguided bird landed behind an island where no-one else could see it, so there was an interval of some minutes before we could add it to the total.

In 1980 we recorded our 100th bird of the day at 08.00, in 1981 at 07.20. Last year we did it in our fastest ever time of 06.22, thus earning ourselves the Barbour Trophy, a sculpture of a Mallard drake by Val Bennett. With the trophy goes a cheque, also donated by Barbour, of £100 to the county naturalists' trust where the 100th bird is found. Thus at 06.20 I checked the score to see how we were doing. With only 91 species recorded, we were still a fair way from the century, but I suppose that 91 species by such an hour is not too bad going.

We left the East Scrape at a jog, rejoined the G and trundled along the beach to the sluice bushes, which the year before had held a delightful Firecrest. (Incidently, I saw my first ever Firecrest in the sluice bushes way back in 1968). This year no Firecrest was there to greet us, but we did see and hear a Lesser Whitethroat, and meet up with Steve Piotrowski, who was anxious to hear what we were missing. 'You haven't got Grey Plover yet?' 'No, no Grey Plover.' 'There's been one flying round all over the place.' 'What about Sandwich Tern – you've got Sandwich Tern?' 'Yes, we got Sandwich Tern ages ago.' Our conversation was suddenly halted by the CB.

Country Life
DAVID TOMLINSON

'Dead Auk to Hawkeye, are you receiving me?' 'Come in Dead Auk.' 'There's two Ruddy Ducks just showing themselves, and the Kingfisher flashed by two minutes ago.' 'Thank you, Dead Auk. We'll be with you in no time.' Dead Auk (alias Mike Trubridge) was manning Island Mere Hide, and the hint of Ruddy Duck galvanised us into action. We leapt into the good old G-wagen, and drove as fast as you decently can on a bird reserve to Island Mere. The G ground to a halt by the rhododendron tunnel; we all tumbled out and set off at a rapid pace for the hide; even Derek broke into a run, which was quite remarkable. Alas, by the time we were in the hide, there was no sign of the ruddy Ruddy Ducks, which had withdrawn back into the reeds. During the breeding season Ruddy Ducks tend to become very secretive, and are much more difficult to see.

Well, the Ruddy Ducks may not be visible, but there was plenty of new stuff to be seen from the hide. Great Crested Grebes were fishing on the mere, while behind them a male Marsh Harrier was quartering the reed bed, our 97th bird at 06.48. There were plenty of other birds to look at as well, with Bearded Tits pinging in

Male Bearded Tit

53

The view from the Island Mere hide at Minsmere. Four Greylag Geese swim across, as a pair of Gadwall loaf among the reeds.

100 species

BARBOUR TROPHY

the reeds, scores of Swifts, Swallows and Martins hawking for insects, and Shoveler, Gadwall and Teal all paddling around. But none of them was new, and it was new birds we needed now for the century.

Nine minutes after the harrier was sighted we picked up a very valuable addition when a fine drake Goldeneye swam into view, later joined by another drake. We thought ourselves lucky in 1982 to see a single female Goldeneye; to see two males was indeed a stroke of luck, and almost made up for the lack of the Ruddy Ducks. I continued to scan the horizon, and was rewarded with the welcome spectacle of a couple of drumming Snipe. You might well think a Snipe is not really a bird to get excited about, but I was tickled pink with those Snipe, for this was a bird we had missed altogether last year. 06.56, and 99 birds recorded – what would be the 100th?

It turned out to be a Yellow Wagtail, sitting on top of a reed and glowing canary yellow in the early morning sun. Early morning sun? Yes, the clouds had parted, revealing brilliant sunshine. So now, at 06.57, we not only had scored our century, but were greatly encouraged by the sun, as welcome a sight as an Osprey or a Black Tern, because it would not be too long before

our Minsmere interlude would be over, and we would be roaring south in the Porsche 911.

Once again the CB burst into life. There was, so we were assured from our helpers on the beach, a Bar-tailed Godwit flying south towards Sizewell. All binoculars focussed to the east, until, with a grunt of satisfaction, we all had it in view, still flying southwards. It was a distant view, but it was a Bar-tail, or at least so we were assured.

Island Mere is often a good place to see Kingfishers, but this morning we were clearly out of luck, though we were fairly optimistic about seeing one later in the day. The winter of '81/82 dealt a bitter blow to the East Anglian Kingfisher population from which they are only slowly recovering.

For a few minutes nothing new appeared, and we were able to sit and enjoy the scene, now bathed in the golden early morning light. The Island Mere hide has long been my favourite at Minsmere, looking south as it does over the reed-fringed mere. I thought back briefly to some of the birds I have watched there over the years, remembering particularly vividly my first-ever Purple Heron which I watched there late one sunlit April evening. It had landed only a few yards

Time 07.00

55

from the hide, of which I was the sole occupant, and as it landed it uncoiled its strangely serpentine neck. I have since watched Purple Herons in many Mediterranean and African countries, and seen them again at Minsmere and at Stodmarsh, in Kent; but none gave the same thrill as that Island Mere bird back in '68.

In my younger days, when I used to stay at Minsmere as a voluntary warden, or 'vol' as they are generally known, Island Mere was my usual destination in the late evening, when great crowds of Swifts, Swallows and martins would fill the sky as they feasted on the evening hatch of midges. Sometimes a Sparrowhawk would try and catch his supper, while invariably the reeds would be full of Bearded Tits (which are never called Bearded Reedlings, as some of the field guides would have you believe, but are usually known as Beardies, which might also be a good collective name for twitchers), and Bitterns would boom as dusk descended.

Alas, the Bird Race seldom allows time for such daydreaming, and it was time to be on the move, perhaps try the sluice bushes again, or give the Scrape another scrutiny, while *I* had still to see a Long-tailed Tit, and none of us had yet scored with either Jay or Marsh Tit. So, somewhat reluctantly, we climbed out of the hide and wandered back to the G-wagen. You might be surprised by the word wandered, but Derek was in the lead, and Derek does not like to be hurried. However, such were the comments from behind his back that Suffolk's county bird recorder was shamed into quickening his pace, breaking into a rather smart gallop which we all attempted to emulate. Back in the G, we bounced our way over the field, which is pock-marked with rabbit holes, housing in turn an army of rabbits.

We were not expecting to see much on this short ride, and we were racking our brains trying to think of what we hadn't seen, when a Kestrel flew past the starboard bow, or the G's offside wing, if you want to be strictly correct. Those of us sitting on the righthand side of the vehicle spotted it without difficulty, those on the left were forced into various contortions before it was seen by all the team. (By some strange twist of fate that Kestrel never had its name added to the list. It would have been bird no. 102, and its absence from the list was only spotted two minutes ago as I wrote this paragraph, a full five days after the event. An extra bird! What on earth will the *ffPS* say when they hear this?)

Replaying my pocket tape player, it is quite apparent why that Kestrel was never noted: seconds after we had all seen it, an urgent call came over the CB: 'Garganey at North Hide!'. Now this was a bird we really needed, and a great shout went up from the G-wagen in anticipation of adding this elusive little duck to our tally. Derek floored the accelerator, and the G bounded down the track towards the North Hide. We passed Steve, who was carefully trailing a pair of Long-tailed Tits. He looked on in astonishment as we sped past him, racing on to the North Hide. We tumbled out of the G almost before it had ground to a halt, and ran furiously to the hide, swallowing mouthfuls of midges on the way. (Swallowing midges is an occupational hazard of running at Minsmere, but I suppose if you swallow enough of them they must give you a calorie or two.)

Kestrel

Sure enough, the Garganey was still there, so close to the hide that at first I overlooked it. It was a very smart drake, dabbling among the mares' tails, and for once we were able to look at it long enough to really enjoy it. Though something of an anti-climax after the Garganey, a Pied Wagtail tripping jauntily along the beach of a nearby island had his name added to the list, and not long afterwards we spotted our first Common Gull. It's high time that the Common Gull was given a new English name, as it's never very common in England, least of all in the spring and summer months. The sun was still shining, but a cool wind was blowing into the hide, so we decided not to linger any longer.

105 species

We made our way back up the track from the car park to Jeremy's bungalow, serenaded by Nightingales all the way. Peter spotted a Marsh Tit, which obligingly waited for everyone to see it, and then a Redpoll flew over, its buzzing flight note drawing our attention to it. Contrary to the opinion the *ffPS* mob have formed of the *Country Life* team, we are very fond of our grub, and we paused briefly to refuel, and load the two cars with the hampers of goodies that would keep us going during the day.

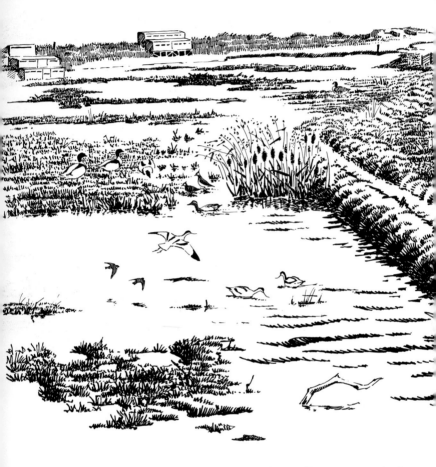

While Jan supervised the loading, we munched our way through croissants and marmalade, and made a mental note of the various food packages that were being packed away. Smoked-salmon sandwiches, pâté en croute, asparagus and ham-stuffed pancakes, prawn and egg mayonnaise rolls, sweetcorn quiche, sausage and apple plait, Scotch eggs, Kendal mint cake, chocolate oliver biscuits, plus numerous Mars bars (a good stand-by, the Mars bar – I think they should sponsor us next year) and a couple of fruit cakes of the type that Jan has gained a reputation for. One thing was sure, we wouldn't be going hungry. With my

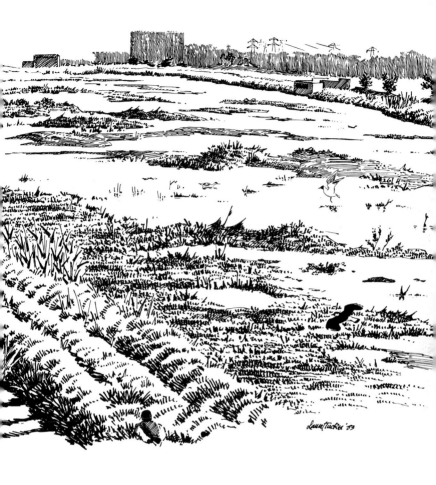

mouth full of bacon roll, I slipped behind the wheel of the Porsche and turned the key: the flat six engine roared instantly into life, ready for the off. For the first time the entire team fitted into the Porsche, Jeremy and Peter in the back, Bill Urwin in the co-driver's seat and myself behind the wheel. It was not quite as tight a fit as we had feared, and my early worries about whether we would all get in were quickly dispelled.

Our first drive in the Porsche would only be a short one, as we were going to make another visit to Island Mere – Mike had just come through on the CB to say that there were now Pochard and Tufted Ducks to be

A panoramic view of the Scrape from the North hide at Minsmere. Mallard, Avocet, Sand Martin, Lapwing, Shelduck, Canada Goose, Moorhen and Black-headed Gull are to be seen; but the star bird is the swimming drake Garganey.

Time 08.00

seen, and he had glimpsed the Ruddy Ducks again. A Jay flew over as we made our way down the track, the Porsche clearly unhappy at trickling along in second gear. The Jay was our 107th bird, on the stroke of 08.00, (though of course if we had noted the Kestrel it would have been no. 108). Last year we had been up to 112 at the same time, an ominous reminder of the poor variety of waders we had recorded on the Scrape.

We jogged back to Island Mere, consuming a few more flies on the way. By now I had changed my wellingtons (green Hunters, of course) for my walking boots, and running was now much less of an ordeal. I had also made the most of the brief interval at the bungalow to take the opportunity to clean my teeth, and it is surprising how such a simple action can revive you. In fact I was feeling much better, ready to start work behind the wheel of the Porsche.

By the time we reached Island Mere for our second visit of the morning the ruddy Ruddy Duck had withdrawn back into the reeds, and nor did we see a Pochard, but we did get the Tufted Duck. The sky was alive with Swifts, and Derek remarked that there really ought to be at least one among them with a white belly. We all turned our attentions to the swifts, but none of us could conjure up an Alpine Swift, nor could we find a Red-rumped Swallow among the numerous hirundines. Time was pressing on, and if we were to leave Minsmere on schedule at 08.30 it was time for us to make a move, so back to the car we went, at a jog once again, and swallowing a few more flies on the way.

110 species

Before we left Minsmere we had one more stop to make, to look for Tree Sparrows, but the G-wagen was to head directly south to Wrenford Forest, where we hoped to find Hawfinch and Firecrest. Before we parted we gave Derek the carbon copy of our scorecard. This was in turn given to Jan, who would be acting as our secretary at base, informing our helpers in Norfolk what birds we still needed, so that they would not waste time looking for birds we had checked off long before.

As expected, our Tree Sparrows proved co-operative, and the convertible Porsche proved its worth, for we all saw them without even getting out of the car. We may have been in for a cold and windy ride, but at least no-one would be complaining that they couldn't see any birds flying over.

One minute after the Tree Sparrow we ticked off Greenfinch, a surprisingly late addition. Last year our first Greenfinch had been no. 62, this year it was no. 112 (all score numbers are now corrected to allow for the missing Kestrel, though of course at the time we didn't realise that we had failed to add it to the list).

We drove slowly past the Little Owl tree, but the Little Owl was playing hard to get, and was probably still sulking at having had the lovers' car parked under his tree for the best part of the night. We couldn't afford the time to search every tree to see if he was watching us from cover, so I turned the Porsche south, through Westleton, and soon the machine was in full cry as I pushed it through the lanes towards Leiston, the big Pirelli P7s gripping the road as tightly as a singing Reed Warbler grasps its perch. Incidently, Pirelli have sponsored the *Country Life* team for the past three years, so it was pleasing that the Porsche was shod with Pirelli rubber.

Although we had seen nearly all the birds we could possibly expect at Minsmere, and felt we had not missed much, there was inevitably the odd one that got away. It was while we were sitting in Island Mere hide that David Bakewell came over the CB from the beach to say that he had four Red-breasted Mergansers in view, flying steadily north. There wasn't much we could do about them. Rather more frustrating was the Pied Flycatcher. It had been seen for the first time the evening before close to the bungalow, but though we looked for it, we failed to locate it, suspecting it of having moved on. Minutes after we had left it was, of course, found again.

Perhaps the most obvious birds missing from our list after leaving Minsmere were Rook and Collared Dove. We soon spied a specimen of the latter perched on a telegraph wire in Westleton, while Rook was added half a mile farther down the road, at 08.32. We had aimed to leave Minsmere at 08.30, so we were running slightly ahead of schedule. Could we keep it up? I know every bend between Leiston and Wrenford, so I was able to use the Porsche's power to its full advantage, the engine howling as I raced up and down through the gears. Fortunately there was little on the roads, and though I was baulked briefly by a dawdling Vauxhall Viva in Snape, we were making impressive

Tree Sparrow

115 species

time. Once we were delayed by a huge container lorry also threading its way through those narrow lanes, but he spotted the Porsche behind him, pulled in and waved us through. Everything was looking good: the sun was still shining, we were well up to schedule, and the only question mark was whether Wrenford would reveal something of its riches to us. We knew that we really needed to get six species here, and these six could make all the difference to the final score. Miss 'em all, and our chances of winning were poor, get the lot and our chances would be greatly enhanced, while such a success would also be a tremendous morale boost so early in the morning.

Of the six species we were banking on finding, we felt fairly certain that Cliff would have alternative sites for three of them on his own patch. He never seems to have any difficulty with Hawfinch (the week before Jeremy and I had looked for his Hawfinches without success), while he also has a reliable site for Woodlarks in the Dunwich Forest area, along with Crossbills. We were less sure about his ability to locate the remaining trio – Siskin, Firecrest and Wood Warbler. We were fairly confident about all three, especially as the dynamic duo in the G-wagen had been joined by John Grant, who was reporting the event for the *East Anglian Daily Times*. Perhaps reporters are meant to remain impartial, but John had agreed to share some of his intimate knowledge of Wrenford Forest with us, and he did know exactly where the Firecrests (two pairs) were singing, and the area most favoured by the Hawfinches.

Back in the Porsche, we were discovering that topless travel wasn't quite as freezing an experience as we might have expected. What was more pleasing was the discovery that we could even talk to each other, though our various styles of windproof headgear, ranging from my sheepskin deerstalker to the balaclavas favoured by Bill and Jeremy, did reduce our hearing to a certain extent. Nor was it surprising that we were not feeling the cold, as we were all pretty well wrapped up, our smart navy-blue *Country Life* sweat shirts buried under a layer of insulated waistcoats, covered with the inevitable Barbour jacket, so we were all the same smart matching shade of Barbour green. This year Barbour had fitted us out with lightweight Durham jackets, which proved ideal. In the car they were windproof, while being lightweight and unlined they were just the job for a breezy May day when a more traditional Barbour would have been too heavy. Barbours also have one other essential advantage, missing from many cheaper waterproof jackets – when you move in them, they do not snap, crackle and rustle, and thus cut out or reduce one's ability to listen for bird song.

For the first few hours of the day we had been concentrating so hard on finding birds we had not had much of an opportunity to discuss the threat posed by the opposition. I admitted to a slight feeling of unease, as this year we had no surprise weapon or tactic, and we could be reasonably certain that they would have followed our example and be using radios for their back-up team. There was even the distinct possibility that they would upstage us and use a helicopter themselves – what an awful thought. Bill Urwin and I had called round at Angel Cottage the afternoon before, and had been somewhat taken back by the presence of a long-wheelbase Land Rover with the words ROYAL AIR FORCE emblazoned in big bold capitals along one side. (We were to recall that Land Rover later when Cliff accused us of turning the Bird Race into a military exercise!) Now what on earth were they doing with the Royal Air Force? This strange alliance between *ffPS* and the Royal Air Force hinted very strongly to me that the old gentlemen would be taking to the air, leaving us playboys (or is it players?) firmly on the ground. This was just too awful a thought to contemplate: the *Country Life* team being upstaged by that lot! I knew that their Saab Turbo, quick as it was, could not hope to keep up with our 911 when driven in anger, but a helicopter could not only blow off the Porsche, but even blow it off the road.

Defeat is one word that doesn't enter into the *Country Life* vocabulary: we had beaten them before and we would beat them again. However, we had come as close to losing last year as it is possible to do, while the year before they had even taken the lead in the late afternoon, only to succumb to our fistful of aces at Snettisham. We had underestimated them in the past: were we doing so again this year?

Bill Urwin and I then recounted for the second time (or it could even have been the third time) our experiences at Angel Cottage the afternoon before. We had been greeted warmly by Robbie Chapman and Cyril Walker (have to admit, albeit reluctantly, that there are some members of the opposition's entourage whose company I actually enjoy! I'm even trying to get Cyril to switch allegiance to us next year, but have yet to come up with a big enough transfer fee) but had not been invited into the cottage. Was there no-one at home? Surely there was, for all the cars were there. Trying not to be rude to Robbie and Cyril, we peered past them into the dark depths of the cottage, and there, sure enough, was the entire *ffPS* team, complete with a dozen or so helpers, evidently discussing tactics. 'Cum inn', said Cliff, his accent hinting at why he supports a football team from a town called Derby (I always thought that Derby was a horse-race at Epsom). We ducked through the entrance porch and made our way into the room where the planning meeting was taking place, as maps were hurriedly folded and notes pulled out of sight.

As we entered, a sudden hush fell on the assembled company, and not a word was said. I could feel their eyes boring into me as I squinted across the smoke-filled room, noting the steamed-up windows. Still not a word was said, and I broke the silence with a feeble joke. I could feel myself being appraised by those members of their back-up team who had never seen me before – so this was the devious dude from *Country Life*. Even the handsome, debonair, charming (etc) John Gooders seemed subdued by the mass of birders, while I never managed to count how many of them there were in that room. I backed out as quickly as I could, not daring to turn my back on them, and made hastily for the door where I was able to fill my lungs with clean air. With so many cigarettes being smoked by the occupants of the room, it would have been appropriate for them to be sponsored by a tobacco company. None of the *Country Life* team, including Jan our chef/secretary and Derek and Steve, smokes, and I suspect it is this extra fitness of being non-smokers that allows us to jog from bird to bird. However, it is a bit difficult to claim that we have no vices while all of us are very partial to the products of two of our major sponsors, Moet & Chandon and Martini.

Our previous week's practice run in the Sierra had

Dude: an amateur birdwatcher, not much good at identification in the field.

taken 20 minutes from Minsmere to Wrenford, and the Porsche only shaved a couple of minutes off this time. We had covered the ground so quickly we were a little worried that we might have beaten the G-wagen, which, being a diesel, was not particularly fast, but when we reached Wrenford there it was, waiting for us. A quick exchange of words with Derek – no, we didn't get Little Owl – and we followed John along the footpath into the forest, surrounded by huge, ancient hollies and gnarled oak trees. We walked in single file, keeping as quiet as possible, and trying not to step on dead twigs or rustle too many leaves. Suddenly, John stopped, and lifted his hand. We all stood still and listened, and sure enough, there was the Firecrest singing away. I had learnt the Firecrest's song in France the year before, so despite my unmusical ear, I knew exactly what to listen for: very similar to that of a Goldcrest, but simpler, and without the Goldcrest's twitter at the end. Smiles all round, and Jeremy pencilled in 08.52 Firecrest. Now this was where we also hoped to find Hawfinch, so we crept a little farther into the wood, listening carefully for the Hawfinch's robin-like *tick*, an easy note to pick up if you know what you are listening for.

As we stood there, listening for the Hawfinch, I re-called the ease with which we had seen them the year before. Steve Piotrowski had been waiting for us at another favourite Hawfinch site, just a few hundred yards from where we were waiting now, in company with the television crew who were filming us that day. Steve had heard Hawfinches, so he whispered to the film crew not to make a sound, as Hawfinches are very shy birds and might well fly away. Seconds later we roared up in the Porsche with much squealing of tyres and revving of engines. Steve was in such a state of suspense he could barely stand it, and looked at us aghast as we all scrambled out of the car. As if on cue, the Hawfinches then flew low over our heads. Within 30 seconds we were on our way, leaving the film crew staring at us in stunned disbelief, though they had managed to film the incident, which later appeared in *The Great Bird Race*.

It was difficult to believe that this luck with such a difficult bird could be repeated a second year, and hopes rose, only to be dashed, when we heard a Starling ticking away for all the world like a Hawfinch. But then

Firecrest

A Hawfinch flies in woodland at 'Wrenford'.

we heard it – there really *was* a Hawfinch ticking away in the tree above us. Nobody else but me saw it, but I had a brief view of its dumpy, short-tailed silhouette and flashing white wing bars as it flew through a gap in the overhead canopy. We had got Hawfinch! So, only three minutes after Firecrest, another vitally important bird was safely out of the way.

We jogged back to the cars, where my navigator Bill had a brief discussion with Derek over our planned route. We were now only a mile from our Woodlark/Crossbill/Siskin site, and we knew where to go there, but we were less certain of the next stop. 'Now listen,' said Derek, 'now just listen. We're going straight to Wrenford Heath . . . No, we'd better not, 'cos you don't know where to go . . .' It turned out we did know where to go, so we parted company with the G, and raced through the forest to the clearing where the Woodlarks were.

The previous year the Woodlarks had led us a merry dance in our efforts to locate them: this year we knew

exactly where to find them. Sure enough, without even leaving the road (though we did all climb out of the car) we spotted a party of four Woodlarks, with the added bonus of a Tree Pipit. So another success, with not a minute wasted. Back in the car we went, with just a half mile drive to our next site.

Time 09.00

Crossbills are strange birds, for their diet of pine-cone seeds seems to give them a constant thirst, for they drink frequently. (Some experts don't think they drink, but come to pools to wash the resin from their beaks. Whatever the reason, they frequently come to water.) Now our next stop was a drinking pool in the forest, a magical spot that, in dry weather, acts as a magnet to birds from miles around. Unfortunately the preceding weeks had been anything but dry, so we were not too optimistic about finding our quarry there.

Here at the drinking pool we did have two helpers already in position – Barry Lawson and Peter Catchpole – and as soon as we arrived they confirmed that we were in luck. Crossbills had been buzzing round all

67

morning, and yes, there was one in that tree right now, a nice, bright-red cock.

It is one of those strange things that sometimes the most obvious birds are the hardest to see. Peter, who is as quick to spot a bird as any of us, could not locate the bird, try as he would. 'Now you see that bare branch to the left?' 'Yes', agreed Peter, 'Then follow it where it meets the trunk of the tree behind and you can't miss it.' Peter still couldn't see it. 'You must be looking at it!' exclaimed Bill Urwin. Peter still couldn't see it. Then, after what seemed like five minutes but was probably less than one, Peter gave a triumphant shout, and Crossbill was added to the list at 09.06.

Peter's difficulty in spotting the Crossbill had at least given me a chance to have a decent look at it, as a good male Crossbill is a fine sight, and one I really enjoy.

No sooner had Peter seen the Crossbill than a small flock of green females flew over, calling *chip-chip-chip*, a very easy note to remember. Then a small bird flew across to the right. Up with the binoculars, but too late to be sure, though it must have been a Siskin. Everyone agreed it must have been, but we needed a better view

if it was to go down on the list. Then another pair flew into view, uttering the flight-call that confirmed them without doubt as Siskins. Where possible, I always like to see birds as well as hear them, and as if wanting to confirm that they really were Siskins, this delightful pair of birds landed close by, in full view. Siskin, 09.07.

We had got both the birds we wanted in no time at all, so it was time to be on our way once again, leaving behind this superb spot, which not only had the two birds we wanted, but was also full of singing Garden Warblers and Blackcaps, a single Nightingale and a pair of Spotted Flycatchers. What was more, the sun was still shining. With a shout of thanks to Peter and Barry, we set off for our next rendezvous with the G-wagen, delighted with our success so far. The most difficult birds of the day cleaned up in minutes!

The next mile took us along a narrow track through the forest. It was dark in the forest, for we were closely hemmed in by the dense stands of conifers, while the sky was now threatening rain. Threat or no threat, there was a new mood of buoyant optimism in the Porsche. It was only 09.15, we had only covered 21 miles since leaving Minsmere, and we were already

A Woodlark rises in its song-flight over typical habitat of cleared ground.

up to 120 species (or 121, had we but realised). We turned out of the forest and onto the main road, with a short drive before we met up with the G-wagen once again, standing at the side of the road like a bright red beacon.

Derek was waiting for us, and as we hurriedly left the Porsche and scrambled into the G, Bill Urwin gave Derek a brief run down on what we had seen: 'We got everything. Tree Pipits calling; Woodlarks got up, flew round before we had waited two minutes; then there was Crossbill in top of the tree, Siskin calling coming over.' 'Get Redpoll there?' Queried Derek. 'Done it!' came the chorused reply. 'We did it way back at Minsmere', Jeremy pointed out.

Within seconds we were trundling down a bumpy track to our Whinchat site, leaving Steve looking after the Porsche. Locking a convertible car is rather a waste of time, so I was delighted to discover that Derek had thought of this, and organised a guard for our transport. Whinchats are rare breeding birds in East Anglia, but John had seen the pair we were going to see several times in the past few weeks, and was confident we would soon find them.

After our recent successes, it was asking too much to find the Whinchats, too, so to use modern birdwatching jargon, we dipped out. (By the way, as I suspect Mr Oddie's account will be full of dipping, stringing, crippling and other birding slang, I have decided to spare my reader such language. In any case, we didn't do too much dipping out.) The Whinchats' site was on private land, and though we could see it well enough from a nearby footpath, we were not allowed to go any closer. We watched in anguish as a bloke with binoculars (a birdwatcher, we presumed), walked bang through the middle of the no-go area, though we were half hoping that he might flush the Whinchat.

Though we may have missed the Whinchat, we did see several more Woodlarks at this site, which was an unexpected bonus, even if they were not a new addition to the list. In flight Woodlarks are easy to pick up because they are much shorter in the tail than the Skylark, while their song is one of the prettiest of any British breeding bird. The last 25 years have seen a marked decline in Woodlark numbers, but the tide may have turned, for they now seem to be doing well

Dip: see p. 24
To string: to claim to have seen/heard a species of bird on flimsy or non-existent evidence. A crippler: a term used to describe a bird of which a good and extended view is obtained, and which is rare or beautiful or both.

in Suffolk, with a healthy and expanding population.

I never tire of listening to Woodlarks, but I also get great pleasure from the shivering song of the Wood Warbler, another song that once heard is difficult to forget. Last year we had heard and seen Wood Warblers at Kelling Triangle, a small wood close to Cley, and one of the most reliable locations for this species in East Anglia. The week before, on the recce, we had visited Kelling, but no Wood Warblers were to be heard, so this was one bird we were anxious to find. A mile along the road from the Whinchat site was a picnic park at the edge of the forest, and here we knew there was a Wood Warbler holding territory.

Woodlark

We followed the G-wagen along to the park and listened for those delicious silver notes. No luck, so we left the car and walked a short distance away, seeing Treecreepers and Goldcrests, neither of which we now needed. Then Derek heard it, the Wood Warbler, and within seconds we all did, singing strongly only a few feet from us. No time to look at it, alas, as now we were heading for Landguard Point, near Felixstowe, where we were confident of seeing Black Redstart. I slid the Porsche's tail gently on the loose surface of the car park, then we were back on to tarmac and heading for Woodbridge and the A12, and then east for Landguard.

We did have one short stop on the way, for shortly before Woodbridge the B1084, on which we were travelling, crosses the head of the Deben estuary. This can be a good site for Kingfisher, so we piled out of the car and made a quick check. No luck. There were Shelduck and Mallard feeding on the mud, but no waders and no Kingfishers. We hurried on, as we knew that in five minutes time the level-crossing gates would close and we should be forced to lose five or so valuable minutes. Once again the sun seemed to be winning the battle with the cloud, and it was warm enough for me to strip a couple of layers of clothes off, and stuff them under the bonnet. (Being a rear-engined car, the bonnet provides the luggage space. A bonnet with no engine underneath it comes as quite a shock to most people. Keith Fairclough, at Minsmere, was very much taken aback by it, especially as I had just told him how much the machine cost. 'Twenty-four thousand and they don't even give you an engine!')

A cock Black
Redstart sings
from the top of a
telegraph-pole at
Landguard Fort.

It is a fast road to Landguard, and we were there at 10.00, and within two minutes I had spotted the cock Black Redstart singing from its favourite song post on one of the old fort's chimneys. Mick Wright, the warden of the bird observatory, was waiting for us, and confirmed that there was nothing else of note for us to see. Negative news can be as valuable as positive news: there was no reason to stop at Landguard any longer, so back in the car onto the A45, then across the new bridge over the Orwell (an invaluable timesaver) and across to Suffolk's southernmost corner in search of Corn Buntings.

This year, for the third time, Daragh Croxson of Radio Orwell covered the Birdwatch, and his first report was due out at 10.00. We switched on the radio, endured the boring old news, and waited for Daragh (whom we had already met earlier in the morning at Minsmere). Reception was not too good at the speed at which we were travelling, but at last we heard Daragh's voice: 'After a dismal start, both sides now on course for that cash target. [The announcer had explained that the Birdwatch hoped to raise £5,000 for

wildlife charities]. Torrential rain [it wasn't torrential, but we had to allow Daragh a bit of journalistic licence] in the early hours made it a miserable start to the morning . . . The *Country Life* team, setting out to beat their own record of 153 species, started birdwatching, or more precisely bird listing, at midnight, and despite that overnight downpour, they were rewarded with one of Britain's rarest breeding birds, Savi's Warbler, and with Minsmere's warden Jeremy Sorensen in their team, they reached the 100 mark at that reserve just before 07.00 this morning.' We knew all this already, how about the other mob? But Daragh went on 'a total that included another rarity, Garganey . . . Their rivals, the *Fauna and Flora Preservation Society* Team . . .' we lost reception for a moment, then heard 'their total of around 110 includes two of Britain's shyest species, Long-eared Owl and Hawfinch . . .' and that was all we heard. So they had got the owl, and Hawfinch. One up to them, but not too much to worry about. After missing Corn Bunting last year, this was one bird that they would be trying very hard for. It was also our next target.

If you know a Corn Bunting site, then this is one of the easiest birds to find, for the males like to sit high on a prominent perch, and sing their happy song, which sounds very much like a jangling of keys. Derek had sorted out a Corn Bunting site for us; we drove straight there, following his careful directions, and I duly beat the rest of the team to spot the Corn Bunting sitting on the top of a telegraph pole. With Corn Bunting out of the way, we had a short interval while we waited for the arrival of the G-wagen, which had been checking out nearby Alton Water while we were looking for the Black Redstart.

It was at Alton that our only back-up team failure took place. The young man who had kindly agreed to check out Alton for us (and who shall be nameless) managed to run out of petrol on his way there, so Derek, Steve and John had to check it themselves. The week before there had been Hoopoe and Black Tern; this week nothing. However, we enjoyed the interval waiting for the G-wagen to report to us. The sun was pleasantly warm, despite the crowds of threatening clouds, and we even managed to see a partridge which looked very much like a Chukkor. Not worth noting for the list, but interesting, nonetheless. We also managed to demolish the pâté en croute, and find the prawn and mayonaise rolls, so our time was not wasted. Suitably refreshed and refuelled, we climbed back into the Porsche, aiming cross-country to the A12, then to the A1100.

Though closely related to the Red-legged Partridge, the Chukkor is not a wild, or even feral (see p. 15) bird in Britain.

By the side of the A1100 there are a number of gravel pits, one of the few reliable sites for Little Ringed Plovers in Suffolk. This should have been a quick job, so we leapt out of the car, grabbed a 'scope, and spent the next five minutes looking for the elusive bird. Peter was on form here, and soon spotted a Common Sandpiper, which we still needed, and he followed this up with a Ringed Plover. The latter was inspected carefully, for though it should have been a Little Ringed Plover, there was always a chance it could be an ordinary Ringed Plover. Bill wasn't very keen on the look of it, and when we got Jeremy's 30 × 60 Optolyth 'scope focussed on it we could see it had orange legs, a colour no self-respecting Little Ringed Plover would be seen dead with. Gloom. There must be a Little Ringed Plover out there.

125 species

There was, and I am pleased to say I found it, on the far side of the pit. (For more distant work I had the slight advantage of using the most powerful binoculars: Leitz 10 × 40 Trinovids. Leitz, as one of our sponsors, had equipped the entire team with Trinovids. Bill Urwin and Peter were using 8 × 40, and Jeremy his own 8 × 32. I have no doubt at all that Leitz do make the finest binoculars you can buy, only rivalled by another West German firm beginning with Z. As the *ffPS* lot were sponsored by the latter, I will say no more, except to repeat the amusing words I had received in a letter from the man at Leitz: 'by using our binoculars I am sure that you will see more birds than your rivals'; I hoped we wouldn't have to disappoint him, as he would have blamed us, not the binoculars!)

With Little Ringed Plover in the bag, there was only one more bird we needed here: Grey Wagtail at a nearby mill. We had never before succeeded in finding a Grey Wagtail on a Record Birdwatch day, so if we did so this year it would be a major accomplishment. Despite the fact that we were running slightly ahead of schedule, our man-on-the-spot, Philip Murphy, was waiting for us in Paper Mill Lane. (As we turned into the lane, Peter, who had never been here before, read the name of the lane out loud, then asked 'What's up here?' With simple northern logic, Bill Urwin replied 'paper mill.' No further comment from Peter.)

Philip greeted us with a smile. 'Yes, I saw one less than 15 minutes ago.' So we followed him along the river bank, at last picking up a Long-tailed Tit – the one bird everyone else had seen or heard except me – on the way. Philip started to look worried, as not a wagtail was to be seen, but then one jumped from the side of the river, and at 11.02 Grey Wagtail joined the tally. Thanking Philip for his help, we set off for our next destination, Livermere, north of Great Barton and on the edge of the Brecks.

It is probably better to be discreet about how quickly we covered the distance from the mill to Bury, but it was dual-carriageway the whole distance, and the Porsche simply ate the miles. When you remember that at 70 m.p.h. a 911 has more than 75 m.p.h. left in hand, you realise what its potential is. At 11.30 we parked the Porsche at Great Livermere, and trotted down the track to meet Tim Brand, who once had the misfortune

Little Ringed Plover (*above*) and Ringed Plover

Time 11.00

75

Egyptian Geese
at Livermere

Egyptian Geese
at Livermere

130 species
131 species

to try and teach me maths. Tim soon confirmed the worst: no Ruddy Ducks; though there was probably a pair present somewhere on the mere, he hadn't seen any. However, there were a few compensations. Egyptian Goose and Pochard were new for us, and there was a feral Barnacle Goose, and a Blue Snow Goose, in with the Canada Geese. So Livermere boosted our total by three; it had also given us plenty of exercise, as it is at least half a mile from the mere to where we had left the car, and we all got very hot running from mere to car, for we were wearing clothes more suitable for high speeds in an open car rather than going for a jog.

Before leaving Livermere we phoned Jan at base to see what news she had for us. Snettisham was a must, with a promise of Red-breasted Merganser, Grey Plover, Knot, Sanderling and Great Grey Shrike. Titchwell was rumoured to have a Baird's Sandpiper, a rare North American vagrant that would have been a new bird for me had I seen it, while at Cley there were stints (both sorts) and a Kentish Plover. So the prospects looked good, and with the sun shining ever more brightly, we were feeling good. Our next stop was Brandon Country Park; our quarry, Golden Pheasant.

Derek, Steve and John had arrived at Brandon well before us, and had enjoyed a well-earned rest in the sun, listening, to quote Derek, 'to the rare sound of continuous calling Golden Pheasant. Fortunately the team arrived before the latter stopped shrieking.' We didn't have such a long rest at Brandon as the back-up, and after hearing the Golden Pheasant, were off again for Weeting Heath, a Norfolk Naturalists' Trust reserve where Stone Curlews breed.

By now we were over half way through the day, with our score standing at 132. (At the same stage in 1982 we were on 133.) We had managed to catch a snatch of Daragh's latest report, the most interesting snippet being the news that *ffPS* had missed the Kentish Plover at Benacre. Not everyone in the car heard this pleasing piece of information, and the conversation went like this. Me: 'They've dipped out on the Kentish.' Bill Urwin: 'They have?' Me: 'They missed it.' Bill Urwin (sounding incredulous): 'They didn't get it?' Me (shouting): 'NO!'

Weeting Heath and the Stone Curlew took no more than two minutes at the most, and soon the Porsche and its driver were relishing the fast and empty roads

132 species

133 species

that were taking us rapidly into North Norfolk, and we were quite delighted when, at 12.50, a pair of Grey Partridges skimmed over the car – if we hadn't had a convertible car would we all have seen them?

Our next destination was an unscheduled extra: a trip of Dotterels had been found in a field near Ringstead a few days before, and our man in Norfolk, Chris Durdin, had checked that they were still there earlier in the day. If we could find these it would be a very useful addition to our tally, so with hopes high and

fingers crossed we turned off in search of them. Bill Urwin had seen the birds earlier in the week, so he knew exactly where to go, but I was somewhat surprised not to find the inevitable line of twitchers scrutinising the Dotterel through telescopes. In fact there was not a single twitcher to be seen. Had the birds flown?

We stopped and swept the fields for a sight of the elusive Dotterel, but to no avail. The huge, rolling

See picture on p. 145

fields looked big enough to lose a flock of Great Bustards, never mind Dotterels, so our lack of success didn't really surprise me very much. Another twitcher turned up, but he couldn't see them, either. We left him to it, but stopped for a last look. A sudden cheer from Bill

Urwin, and there they were: four immaculate Dotterels running round on the winter wheat. It would have been nice to sit down and watch them for a while, but time was pressing, and we were overdue at Snettisham. I pulled myself away from the Dotterels reluctantly, fired up the Porsche, and backtracked to Snettisham.

Good old Derek was waiting for us when we arrived

at Snettisham, enjoying a snooze in the G-wagen after dropping Steve and John off at the beach. Snettisham's road is much better suited to a tough cross-country vehicle than a Porsche, so once again we switched vehicles for the ride down to the beach.

Now Snettisham fills the *Country Life* team with mixed emotions. In 1981 it produced the flurry of good birds we needed to win the day; in 1982 we wasted so much time there we very nearly lost because of it. This year it proved invaluable once again, thanks to the help of its warden, Pete Gotham. Pete soon told us what was around and what we had missed, and amazed me when he said that there was still six or seven hundred Brent Geese out on the Wash. Steve and John had seen the Brent, but we were not so lucky, though we did see several sparkling Grey Plover in fresh spring plumage out on the mud. (Is there a more splendid wader in spring finery than a Grey Plover?)

While we were still looking for the Brent, Steve went in search of Whinchat, soon finding one and calling us over with the CB. Whinchat joined the list at 14.25, 25 minutes later than Grey Plover – had we really wasted all that time looking for Brent? Before leaving, at Derek's insistence, we gave them one last try, and John managed to pick up a pair in his 'scope. We each queued for a view, before hurrying back to the G-wagen. Derek then ferried us back to the Porsche; we left to go to Hunstanton in the hope of a wader or two on the beach, or perhaps an Eider out to sea; the G was to go on to Cley.

136 species
Time 14.00

137 species

138 species

Grey Plover at Snettisham

Two Little Gulls, one flying and one swimming, lose themselves in a flock of Black-headed Gulls at Titchwell; Swifts hawk for insects behind them.

Time 15.00

139 species
140 species

141 species

At Hunstanton we drew a blank – or not quite a blank, because we met up with Chris Durdin, who had plenty of useful information for us. As we had to pay to enter the cliff-top car park, we tried to get our money's worth with a quick seawatch. We soon located a small party of Common Scoter well offshore, and enjoyed better views than we had had at Minsmere all those hours ago, while stiff-winged Fulmars glided past within inches of us. But we didn't need to see any more Fulmars, either, so back into the car and on to Titchwell.

Titchwell is one of the RSPB's greatest success stories, and on a good spring day it is an entrancing place to spend an afternoon. However, we weren't there to be entranced, but to seek what we hadn't already seen. We broke into a gentle trot along the wall, soon noting a trio, if not more, of Little Gulls, and our first Little Grebe of the day. We were now up to 140 species at 15.27, having reached Titchwell an invaluable two hours earlier than the previous year. A distant Sanderling joined the list at 15.27, and ten minutes later Peter

spotted a couple of ducks on the sea, only to lose them again. I found them in my scope – a Bushnell Spacemaster with 22× wide angle – and was soon able to diagnose them as Eider, my identification speedily verified by the rest of the team. We set back at a run for the car.

142 species

The rumoured Baird's Sandpiper had long since disappeared, but as we jogged back, panting for breath in the hot sun, we met a crowd of twitchers coming the other way, following up a report that the Baird's was in the far corner of the marsh. Should we try for it or not? I was dead set against it, but Bill Urwin argued that it was worth it, 'we've still got hours . . . at least another five hours' daylight'. I pointed out that time was slipping away at a great pace, and that no doubt Derek would have everything lined up for us at Cley, only for us to arrive too late to see it. Besides, it wouldn't be long before we came face to face with Oddie & Co. Bill Urwin insisted, and I retorted that 'I'll blame you if we lose.' Weak-willed individual that I am, I gave in, and we trudged back through the energy-sapping soft

Time 16.00

While a Spoonbill
sleeps, a female
Pintail swims in
front of Dawkes
hide at Cley. Both
of these birds were
also seen by the
ffPS team.

sand in search of the fabled Baird's. We didn't see it.

I suppose that the search for the Baird's didn't lose us much more than 20 minutes, but it was a relief to be back at the car, shed some more clothing (it was hot work galloping all round Titchwell), and have a good, long drink of water. Then it was on to Cley, winding our way through the twisting lanes of the North Norfolk coast, through the Burnhams – Burnham Deepdale, Burnham Norton and Burnham Overy Staithe – past Holkham (no need to stop to look for Egyptian Goose), through Wells and Stiffkey. This was where the Porsche came into its own, its powers of instant acceleration and astonishing cornering perfectly suited to the narrow road, with its many good straights, broken up by sharp second-gear corners. Looking back, I am glad I was the driver and not a passenger.

Our two men at Cley – Stuart Betts and Andy Stocker – had been out since 05.30 sorting birds out for us. They had checked on the Dotterels, and had also found no fewer than seven singing Corn Buntings, just in case we still needed one. During the morning they had located Greenshank, Temminck's and Little Stints and Kentish Plover for us, only to have everything scared off at lunchtime by a Crane that flew in from the sea, and then proceeded to circle the marsh. All the migrant waders departed, and so too had the Crane by the time we arrived.

Derek and Co in the G-wagen had arrived at Cley well before us, to be greeted by Roy Robinson at Walsey

Hills on the CB. Roy had everything under perfect control, and the back-up team were able to relax again while Roy directed operations. Shortly before we arrived in the Porsche, the *ffPS* Saab Turbo had arrived on the scene, and the *ffPS* mob were wandering about looking for birds when we roared up, racing straight past Cley and on to Whalsey Hills for our instructions. There were, so we were told, just two birds for us at Cley: Pintail and Spoonbill. We wasted no time in seeing them, and also added White-fronted Goose to our total. It seems very doubtful whether these had been bred in Siberia, or ever flown any further than Holkham, but they were a useful addition to the list, and one that we were amused to discover later had been counted as genuine wild birds by *ffPS*.

Over the CB came our next instructions: there was a Bean Goose down on the Quags. We ran back to the car and accelerated away, rushing past the opposition team as I was just changing up from second to third at 6,000 r.p.m. I glimpsed one of the baddies (in fact it was the goodie), and gave a cheerful hoot. Funny how that lot always look glum. As Cley was evidently their first stop on the north Norfolk coast we were well ahead of them, which must be a good thing.

By now the G-wagen was waiting for us down on the Quags, and we didn't even have to have the Bean Goose pointed out to us. Another escape from a collection? Rather more exciting was the news that Steve had found a Short-eared Owl, but it had just dropped

DAVID TOMLINSON

143 species
144 species
145 species

146 species

147 species
Time 17.00

148 species
Time 18.00

down. We waited a few minutes and it obligingly came up again, and we all saw it. Time 17.00, and time also to leave north Norfolk. Derek promised a White Stork for us if we could get back to Suffolk in time. We left the G to drive to Benacre, where we would next meet it; our route was to take us across north Norfolk to Acle, where Bill Urwin was confident that he could find a Little Owl, then to Breydon for Cormorant, and south to Lound for Kingfisher.

The gap between the Short-eared Owl and our next bird, Bill Urwin's faithful Little Owl, was exactly an hour, an hour of rapid motoring, and tucking into smoked salmon and green pepper sandwiches. We halted briefly in Acle at Bill Urwin's house, where Chris, Bill Urwin's wife, and his two small sons, David and Joseph, were amazed to see us. We refilled the drinking-water bottles and checked with Jan at base. No, there wasn't much for us at Minsmere that we hadn't already got, but the White Stork at Wangford looked safe.

At 18.20 Cormorant at last joined the list, and we

found ourselves in exactly the same spot where we had
been some 17 long hours before. Cormorants are not
birds that I insist on stopping to admire, so with that
out of the way we threaded through Yarmouth's
Saturday evening traffic south to Lound Waterworks.
Last year we had waited 10 minutes for the Kingfisher
to show itself; in contrast this year it only took two. If
we had but known it, this was our 150th species, but
thanks to the forgotten Kestrel, we thought it was the
149th. Ironically, we had seen many more Kestrels,
but it never occurred to us that we hadn't actually put
it on the list.

We still had some rapid motoring to do before we got
to Benacre and parked the Porsche next to the empty
G-wagen. It was now 19.00, but it was a light evening,
with excellent visibility. We trotted along the beach
towards the Broad, looking out to sea in hope of
Gannet, but no joy. Nor did we have any luck with the
CB, for we could get no response from Hawkeye. His
batteries had gone dead.

A Kingfisher
whirrs low over
the water at
Lound.

150 species

Time 19.00

151 species

We arrived at the Broad in the nick of time, for a courting couple had wandered over to the Broad from the beach, and the young man was now aimlessly throwing pebbles into the Broad. Words failed us. Could this be an agent working for the other side? Perhaps it was even the same couple whose car we had found underneath the Little Owl's tree?

His stone-throwing did flush a Greenshank, which we saw and heard as it flew away. Species no. 151, or 150 as we thought at the time. We were well pleased, but Derek, with whom we had now caught up, wasn't. 'What kept you?' he demanded. Having been driving flat out for the last couple of hours, with only brief intervals to tick off Little Owl, Kingfisher and Cormorant, I felt like retorting that it was because our car was so slow, but this was not the time for sarcasm. It turned out that up until three minutes before, a fine adult Mediterranean Gull had been sitting in full view on the Broad, but the rock-chucking antics of the aforementioned young man had scared it off. If only we had been three minutes earlier.

Still, you can't get 'em all, so we trudged back to the cars, learning from David Bakewell and Reg Clarke, who had spent the previous two hours at Benacre, that we had also missed a fishing Osprey.

There was still a chance of a Gannet, as there was a good passage of gulls along the coast, so we sat down for 10 minutes and glassed the sea. No Gannet, though we did have good views of a small flock of Eider, again spotted by Peter.

Now it was the turn of the White Stork to have the privilege of being ticked off by the *Country Life* team, so we followed the G down to Wangford. This White Stork had been present in the area since June 1982, but it was rumoured to have left, with no recent reports of it. However, farmer John Holmes, who is well-known locally for his interest in wildlife, had located the bird on his land, and sportingly 'phoned up Minsmere to let us know that if we wanted to see it, he could probably find it for us.

Our first problem was finding John's farm. We made our way to Wangford, where the G-wagen stopped to ask a girl, leading a smart chestnut pony, the way. Whatever birds they had seen during the day, the moment was the high-light for the occupants of the

G-wagen. It has to be admitted that the young lady did have a remarkably fine figure for one so young, while her tight-fitting jodphurs and somewhat flimsy blouse did set it off a treat. Even so, this was no excuse for the five occupants of the G (and all but one of them married men) to be so stunned as to not take in her reply. We received the distinct impression that they would have rather watched her all evening and forgotten about White Storks.

Fortunately John Holmes's farm was not far away and, furthermore, he was delighted to see us. Within seconds he had his car out of the garage and we were following him along the lane, looking for the stork. We found it within minutes thanks to his help, preening in the evening sun. It was exactly 180 days since I had last seen a White Stork, at Taita Hills in Kenya . . .

152 species

Now there was nothing to do except head back for Minsmere, stopping first of all at the Island Mere to see if those rotten, unsporting Ruddy Ducks had come out to play. No, not a sign of them. Then the CB crackled into life again: there was a Wood Sandpiper outside North Hide. Panic! Another headlong rush to North Hide, just as we had done all those hours before for Garganey. Once again we were successful, with a fine pair of Wood Sandpipers feeding close to the hide at 20.20.

Time 20.00

153 species

Jan was delighted to see us back at Minsmere, as in previous years we had always promised to get back in daylight, but never did so. We gave her a ride in the Porsche (on Bill Urwin's lap) back to the Island Mere, recounting some of our adventures, and hearing her account of the *ffPS*'s visit to Minsmere earlier in the day, which did not sound as if it was a great success. We were greatly amused to learn that a member of the *ffPS* back-up had even mistaken assistant-warden Mike Trubridge for a fellow member of the same team, and had asked him whether John (whoever John was) should be summoned from Island Mere hide. Mike replied no, of course not, adding to the *ffPS* man's confusion.

We stayed in Island Mere until 20.45, then set out for Reydon, where we had seen a Barn Owl the week before. It may have been a long shot, but it was worth a try. In the cool of the evening we left the Porsche at Minsmere, and once again used Jeremy's Volvo.

Time 21.00

We had only been in position a few minutes when Peter gave a shout of triumph – a Barn Owl in sight. Squinting through my Trinovids in the fading light, I saw the ghostly white form quartering a field. For the first time ever we had recorded a Barn Owl on a Bird Race day.

Time 22.00

On our way back to Minsmere we had a half-hearted look for Long-eared Owls, but the inspiration was no longer there, so instead we called it a day and returned to base. Oh the luxury of getting back early! I washed my hair, cleaned my teeth, changed my trousers and felt totally revived, while it was decided that the final touch of one-up-manship would be to type our species

Time 23.00

list. Jan volunteered for this chore, so by 23.00 we had a neatly typed list. After another piece of cake and a coffee or two, we piled into our various wagons for the return to the finish.

Needless to say, the *ffPS* supporters were greatly taken back when we arrived at 23.30 looking smart and relaxed. Worried expressions were quickly exchanged – what on earth were we doing there half an hour early? I handed our score card over to Crispin Fisher, natural history editor of Collins books, who had kindly consented to be our judge, and found myself a drink. With 154 species in the bag – not including Kestrel – we were confident we had done well. If *ffPS* had managed to beat us, they would have done extraordinarily well, as luck had clearly been on our side. However, win or lose, we had enjoyed a super day – the sun had shone, the Porsche had been a delight to drive, and everything had worked to plan. What more can a man ask?

Time 24.00

Well, I s'pose there is one more thing a man can ask, and that is to win. At four minutes to midnight four tired men climbed out of their Saab Turbo and staggered into the cottage. They were not looking too happy, but it was still too early to permit myself a smile. Minutes later Crispin came into the room, and in the style of the Miss World contest, announced the runner-up first: the *ffPS* had scored 145; *Country Life* had scored

155 species

154, a total which included a Montagu's Harrier (sorry, not allowed to reveal where we saw it!). So we had retained the trophy by a handsome margin, even without Kestrel, and with our century before 07.00, we had won the Barbour trophy too. There was only one problem: with such a convincing win, would they want to play with us again? More likely they will suggest a change in the rules ... But one thing was sure – we had gripped them off good and proper!

So once again the dynamic *Country Life* team's quest for perfection had won the day, and a hat-trick of wins in the contest. More to the point, had we set a new record? In 1982 our total of 153 included Blue Snow Goose and Barnacle Goose, and though both are on the official British list, we suspected that they were not genuine wild birds. This year we recorded 155 species, including four species of geese whose origins are suspect – Bean, White-fronted, Barnacle and Blue Snow. We had thus equalled our previous record, and bettered it with the addition of those four species of geese. However, it can also be argued that all four have more claim to be included in our total than Egyptian Goose. The latter falls into category C of the British list, which means that 'although introduced by man, it has now established a regular feral breeding stock which apparently maintains itself without necessary recourse to further introduction'. As it is impossible to interview the geese we saw, and request them to reveal where they were born, it seems easier to add them to the total. So yes, we had set a new record for a one-day sponsored birdwatch in England, and 155 is the total we will try and beat next time.

In conclusion, it has to be admitted that the '*Country Life* Record Birdwatch' is not an event of ornithological significance, even if it does provide a barometer of population trends and so on. However, its greatest justification is that it provides a lot of fun for many people, and raises very worthwhile sums for wildlife conservation. The full list of the sponsors of both teams appears on page 153. The money raised has gone to a variety of projects, including the RSPB's woodland bird survival campaign; the World Pheasant Association; the Norfolk Naturalists' Trust; the Suffolk Trust for Nature Conservation; Landguard Point Bird Observatory; and of course the *ffPS*'s 100% Fund, which helps finance numerous conservation projects all over the world. Since its inception in 1980, the '*Country Life* Record Birdwatch' has raised more than £13,000 for wildlife conservation: we think this justifies the event's existence, and I hope you agree.

Country Life
DAVID TOMLINSON

To grip somebody off: to see/hear a species which he does not.

Barn Owl

John Gooders
(*Photo P. R. Crabb*)

Bill Oddie
(*Photo P. R. Crabb*)

THE *ffPS* TEAM

Cliff Waller
(*Photo B. R. Ivison*)

Tim Inskipp
(*Photo Robbie Chapman*)

The Account of the Fauna and Flora Preservation Society team

BILL ODDIE

I AM WRITING THIS ON OUTSKERRIES – a tiny island, part of the Shetland group, hundreds of miles north of Minsmere. I have now seen 62 species of birds during the past 5 days. There are no other bird-watchers here to confirm my sightings, nor to question them. I can't be 'gripped off', and I can't 'dip out', because if *I* don't see what's here, nobody else will! There's absolutely no 'competition'. This, to me, is ideal birding. It's the very antithesis of and the perfect antidote to a 'Big Bird Race'. Aren't I lucky!? Be that as it may . . .

Grip, dip: see pp. 89 and 70 respectively

I was first contacted about 'Bird Race 1983' sometime back in autumn 1982. John Burton, our tireless organiser, and the most selfless megalomaniac I know, rang to say that he would in fact *not* be marshalling the *ffPS* campaign this year. I was summoned to a pub 'somewhere near London Zoo' to meet the new regime. They were all distinguished associates of World Wildlife Fund, the British Museum or other active conservation concerns: some I knew, some I didn't. Mark Carwardine and Tim Parmenter would have the unenviable task of persuading sponsors to put their money on our birds, under the overall leadership of Cyril Walker. Cyril was a 'tick' for me. At this meeting he seemed energetic, efficient and optimistic. I was to talk to him many times on the 'phone over the following months. He frequently sounded weary and depressed; probably because he often was. If you've ever tried hustling sponsors you'll know why. Many million-pound high-profit-margin business concerns will happily squander a hundred thousand quid on filming a lousy commercial in Barbados that ends up looking like it was shot in Torquay; but try tapping them for 'a pound a bird' and they'll bleat on about 'recessions and cut backs'. These folks will spend more on a business lunch than it would take to save the Mauritius Kestrel. By spring '83 Cyril had a file of refusals from several hundred companies ranging from oil magnates to hamburger kings.

Nevertheless our team were tireless; and not all companies are stingy. Many were very generous and as the date approached it became clear that Cyril's fund-raising operation had guaranteed that we would raise something near £3,000, to be divided between the Royal Society for the Protection of Birds, the Wildfowl Trust and the local conservation groups of East Anglia whose land we were to invade.

The onus was now on us, the birding team, to justify such support. We certainly wanted a good score, and, be honest, it'd be nice if we actually won!

The first decision was – transport. We didn't really want to compete with David Tomlinson's jet-propelled Porsche, though in the past we'd almost tried. In 1981 our Aston Martin – lovely virility symbol though it was – had proved somewhat unsuited to the task, having only two doors, the visibility of a submarine (to those of us in the back) and a road clearance that would barely straddle a matchbox. The 1982 super Range Rover, with extra length, was in many ways an ideal vehicle. Ideal to ride in anyway; but John was the driver and in fact he'd found 24 hours of giant Rover manoeuvring had developed his arm muscles out of proportion to his otherwise immaculately designed body. We *could* have the Range Rover again in 1983 – or we could have a Saab Turbo, via a mutual contact of David Tomlinson and myself. What's more, Saab would let us have not only this superb car, but also a back-up vehicle, *and* a driver, *and* sponsor us as well. It was thus hardly relevant that John preferred to drive the Saab anyway. The car was duly delivered to my London home two days before the race, and by the time I'd driven it to Suffolk I was so enamoured of it that I volunteered to take over the driving for the race itself! The Saab turned out to be one of the major successes of the day – fast and comfortable, plenty of room, great visibility and four doors for birdwatchers to tumble out of at maximum speed.

So, we had Cliff's Land Rover for the early morning

rough stuff and the Saab for the long road journeys. We also seemed to have the offer of a helicopter! A gentleman high up in the RAF was not only an acquaintance of Cyril Walker's but also an avid birder. Cyril rang with the news and the enquiry . . . 'What do you think of going to Holland early on the day'?! I thought only for a moment before countering: 'Well . . . how would we feel at the end of the day if we discovered *Country Life* had flown to Holland?' . . . I answered my own question . . . 'I *think* I'd think it was cheating'. Or at least 'ungentlemanly'. There was actually nothing in the rules to say we were restricted to *British* Birds, but I'm sure it was assumed. We could, of course, ask David Tomlinson if a European jaunt was allowed but then we'd be admitting we'd got a helicopter which, knowing his competitive spirit and impressive contacts, would no doubt inspire him to hire Concorde and visit Panama for an hour or two between Minsmere and Cley. Anyway, I argued, I really felt we'd done pretty well by pottering along on our own path in previous years, and nipping to Holland might totally disrupt what little routine we'd developed. Long before I'd finished arguing with myself, Cyril had agreed. Did we want the helicopter at all then? I called John Gooders and we soon resolved that the best use of a 'chopper' would be to board it at lunchtime, after we'd got a firm base to our score in Suffolk, and fly as far north as possible to try and tick off the several seabirds we usually missed. Yorkshire or even Northumberland perhaps – for Razorbill, Guillemot, Puffin, Gannet, Shag, maybe Rock Pipit and hopefully Eider and scoter on the sea from the air. In fact we may not have to land at all before dropping back down in North Norfolk by about 16.00, picking up the car again and carrying on our 'usual' route. It was probably a good plan as it was exactly what the RAF man suggested himself. He'd worked out how long it would take to Bempton Cliffs in Yorkshire and back and was looking forward to the race. The helicopter would surely also attract sponsors, especially if we could tow a hamburger-shaped barrage balloon . . . or maybe even an oversized Sunday Newspaper . . . or an inflatable female celebrity? In any event it looked likely to add maybe half a dozen birds to our score during a period we traditionally 'wasted' driving up through East

Anglia. Of course it all fell through. Despite the determination and rank of our RAF man some red-tape department tied up the helicopter's blades, claiming it was not what RAF transport was really meant for. We couldn't argue with that. It *was* a bit of a blow, but sort of what we'd come to expect. Nevertheless, the RAF man was determined to help and he did . . . as you shall read anon.

Meanwhile . . . on 30th April, two weeks before the race, I tried to organise an informal 'planning meeting'. I had to visit Norwich for an RSPB members' 'do', so I travelled on to Suffolk and met up with Cliff Waller. John Gooders was, alas, unable to make it, and Tim Inskipp would have had too long a journey – he was in Botswana. Last year Cliff had had rather a hard time just before the race; his house had partially flooded, he'd had little sleep and many of the birds he'd 'staked out' had disappeared. On the 30th, I found him in much better spirits. He and his assistant warden had already begun searching for 'difficult species' and, even more to the point, he was clearly working himself into a mood of amiable competitiveness.

Checking out birds two weeks before the date can easily lead to misplaced optimism – they *do* have a habit of slipping away during the following fortnight. However, we couldn't resist making a bone-shaking 'recce' in Cliff's Land Rover round some of his favourite haunts. We visited a 'secret' marsh and saw Spotted Redshank, Garganey and Snipe – all often difficult birds on the day – and Cliff explained his intention of dropping the water levels on some of his reserve pools nearer the time to attract more waders. The ability to create wader habitat could prove particularly valuable as the water at Minsmere, so often the haunt of a host of spring waders, was particularly high. However, there were Goldeneye, Jack Snipe and Mediterranean Gull there – which we hoped might hang on for a couple more weeks. Benacre Broad sounded a good bet too: Long-tailed Duck still there. As Cliff and I toured the marshes we no doubt both felt quietly confident, but *Country Life* have an uncanny knack of unnerving their opposition – their shadows are long, and they are everywhere. It must be like being 'tailed' by a private detective. Even as we strolled through the reed-beds two weeks before the race four distant heads popped up half a mile away. Cliff whispered: 'The Suffolk lads . . . Tomlinson's back up boys . . . probably checking out Savi's.' Then he waved cheerily to let them know we'd seen them, and to indicate he wasn't perturbed. *I* was.

We also had news of *Country Life*'s ever-advancing technology. A local reporter had asked Cliff if he could keep in touch with us during the race. Cliff had explained it was difficult as our moves were unpredictable. 'Can't you radio through to us?' the reporter

The approximate final route of the *ffPS* team (based on an Oxford University Press map)

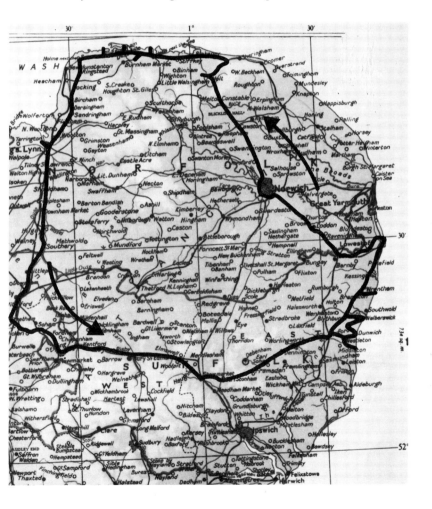

asked. 'Radio . . . *what* radio?' 'You've got CB radio on Whalsey Hill in North Norfolk haven't you?' . . . We hadn't, but clearly *Country Life* had. I comforted myself by arguing that if *I* was chasing birds in Suffolk I'd be positively aggravated to be told over the radio 'get up to Cley immediately, there's a Hen Harrier flying over.'

We also heard David Tomlinson wanted to change the start rule to 'within 35 miles of Saxmundham'. We agreed that it didn't matter to us. We also agreed there must be a reason. The rumour was they were going dazzling Kittiwakes at Lowestoft at midnight. Were we right? I must read David's account . . .

On Thursday 12th May John Gooders joined Cliff and they presumably had a day checking out sites, assessing the situation, and planning strategy. The simple fact is that if you're going birding in East Anglia then you have to *live* in East Anglia really to know what's happening. For weeks I'd been making notes on possible routes and problem species; but as I drove the final miles up from London on Friday – the 13th, no less! – I suddenly realised I hardly knew the right road to Minsmere let alone the likeliest spot to hear a Wood Warbler. Cliff lived there, John knew it well and they'd been discussing it all since yesterday. I lived in Hampstead and Tim had only just got back from Botswana – clearly it was over to Cliff and John.

The original 1981 team were re-united at Angel Cottage (Cliff's place) at 15.00 on the Friday. There were happy handshakes and discouraging mutters: 'Not a lot about'. The weather had been stormy during the past week. It was clearer now, sunny almost, but with a stiff south-west wind. There were obviously no migrational movements in progress, nothing much coming in and indeed, with the clear skies, passage birds were probably leaving at that very moment. We predicted a low score.

For the next hour or so it was photo-time: for the impending book, and to prove to our sponsors that we really were flashing their names about. We slipped in and out of T-shirts; dangled our Zeiss binoculars in front of the camera; pretended to talk into our little Sanyo tape recorder; and sprawled over the Saab like models at the Motor Show. At 17.00 we stopped giggling and camping about and trotted off to get down to the serious part of the afternoon: the planning meeting.

This was our first and only *real* planning meeting: an hour, on the eve of the race. However, it was still more elaborate than anything we had done before. For a start we were not alone. In fact the room was packed with half a dozen other birders – amongst them Cyril Walker, Tim Parmenter and brother, Mark Carwardine and even John Burton who, since having announced his non-involvement six months ago, was as involved today as he'd ever been! There were a couple more of Cliff's local friends; a driver from an East Anglian Saab dealer; and at least two RAF chaps sporting regulation moustaches and other impressive equipment – namely, four walky-talkies. Our back-up system and the communication process was explained to us. At first I couldn't quite figure out who was supposed to do what, nor indeed exactly who everyone was. To make sure I never *would* understand we were all given codenames or call-signs or whatever you're supposed to use over walky-talkies. The main *ffPS* team – i.e. us – were supposed to be called 'Corn Bunting', in memory of last year's bogey bird. The result of this was that every time John Gooders said 'Corn Bunting calling' the other three of us nearly had heart failures. It was midday before we stopped asking 'where . . . where?' The main back-up vehicle, the second Saab, piloted by John Burton, was called 'Grouse'. We assumed this was an abbreviation of 'Famous Grouse' (*the* ornithological whisky), patrons of the *British Birds* Bird Photographer of the Year award. Tim Parmenter's call-sign was 'Sun Grebe' – no doubt an abstruse *ffPS* joke that would have tickled them pink at any International Conservation symposium but puzzled me entirely. Tim didn't even *look* like a Sun Grebe – or maybe he did (what *is* a Sun Grebe?) The RAF Land Rover would carry the fourth walky-talky and Cyril Walker. They would be 'Dipper' . . . another ornithological joke, not based we hoped on Cyril's reputation. ('To dip' is birders' slang for failing to see an expected bird. The *ffPS* team are experts at it.)

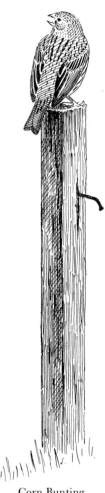

Corn Bunting, the *ffPS* team's bogey bird in 1982

For reasons I couldn't fathom John Burton announced he was there 'to communicate', *not* to find birds – maybe it was his last gesture of non-involvement. He would carry a 'bleeper' like doctors do so they can be called in an emergency. If John was 'bleeped' it would mean hot news had been 'phoned into the cottage from somewhere in East Anglia. John would then find a 'phone-box, get the news and call us on his walky-talky: 'Grouse to Corn Bunting'. As it turned out the bleep only went once on the race day: at 20.30 with news of a bird we'd seen ten minutes before. This was probably just as well, as the walky-talkies generally proved to have such a short range that much of John's 'communication' involved him driving just behind us and yelling out of the car window.

At the planning meeting we assumed all this *Country Life*-like technology would work, though we couldn't help asking why we couldn't use our own names instead of the call-signs. Why couldn't we just say 'This is John calling'? The RAF came up with the correct military explanation: 'Because there's more than one John'. This was true. There were two, and indeed two Tims. Personally I feel it likely that each John or Tim would easily be able to figure out which they were; but no, we had to use the code-names. This may of course have been also to thwart the possibility of *Country Life* tuning in to our wavelength. Now, if they did, they might well be dispirited at the news that we'd already had 'Corn Bunting calling', not to mention 'Dipper', 'Grouse' and 'Sun Grebe'. They'd be convinced we *had* got a plane, if not a spaceship.

By the end of our briefing we were a little concerned that we'd forget who everyone was. We did; but since the walky-talkies failed to work so often it didn't really matter. Anyway, they gave us a lot of laughs and often kept up our morale during the day.

The next stage of the planning meeting was 'Recent Reports and News' and a prospective route. I'd already accepted that my theories were pretty redundant and Tim clearly felt that his recent sightings in Botswana were largely irrelevant. Cliff and John did most of the talking.

In previous years our basic routine had been much the same. Up and out about 03.30 . . . 'night birds' round Cliff's own heathland and dawn chorus and early stuff in 'his' woods and marshes. On to Minsmere by 08.00-ish; an hour or so there; and then back to Angel Cottage for a large cooked breakfast. Late morning we'd trundle up northwards via Lowestoft; then we'd call in at various sites – usually abortively –

on our way up through mid-Norfolk. At about 16.00 we intended to hit Hunstanton, and then we'd work our way along the north Norfolk coast via Titchwell and Holkham, ending up at Cley for the final couple of hours of daylight.

This year several things were to be different. First, we'd be out at 02.00. Still not as obsessive as *Country Life*'s midnight start, but decidedly more 'professional'. Secondly, there would be no breakfast stop . . . we'd carry a liberal stock of sandwiches, fruit, coffee and so on, to be consumed in the car on the move. Thirdly, we wouldn't go to Minsmere till late morning – *after* we'd been to Lowestoft, and we'd leave for Norfolk at about 13.00. The idea was to clear up far more of the difficult local species *before* we set off north. At this point, we would decide which way to do the Norfolk coast: Hunstanton to Cley, or possibly Cley first then work back west. It all sounded much less 'gentlemanly' than previous years. We then discussed a positively horrendous possibility. Should we start at midnight, 35 miles west of Saxmundham as the new rule allowed, and drive to Wicken Fen near Cambridge where a Spotted Crake had been calling nocturnally for the past week or so? Thankfully the idea was quashed (*a*) because Spotted Crakes tend to call less as night wears on and (*b*) because if we missed it we'd be so upset traipsing back to Suffolk for two birdless hours that we might well be tempted to give up and go back to bed. We decided to leave the Wicken trip till dusk when we'd have a chance of not only the Crake but also Hobby, a bird *Country Life* were unlikely to get.

Much of this route was dictated by our 'Recent Reports and News'. It was clear that Cliff had been working very hard indeed. His information was neatly written out on little green cards. Much of it was unfortunately negative: 'Minsmere: water high, very few waders, but Goldeneye and Mediterranean Gull recently.' 'Cley:' the same story 'few waders, but Spoonbill and occasional sightings of Kentish Plover and Temminck's Stint.' 'Benacre Broad:' clearly worth a visit 'Kentish Plover, Little Gull and Med. Gull, tho' Long-tailed Duck has gone.' It was from Benacre we intended to do a bit of a sea-watch and try and pick up some of those passing seabirds now knocked out by the loss of the helicopter. I challenged Cliff with difficult

Drake Goldeneye

species and he responded: Wood Warbler? – not at the usual Norfolk site yet, but he had two singing birds nearer 'home'. Woodlark? – not at last year's site; could be difficult. Nightjar? – probably not arrived yet. Negative news could be useful if it saved us pointless searches. Cliff even had a 'certain spot' for the dreaded Corn Bunting. Nevertheless, no matter how much he divulged I still had a feeling that there were some things Cliff wasn't even going to tell his own team! Presumably he'd *show* us next day instead.

At 17.30 we were making a final attempt to remember who was 'Sun Grebe' and why, when the 'enemy' appeared at the window: the cheeky, hairy, if curious, face of Bill Urwin, and behind him the immaculately groomed, felt-capped David Tomlinson, looking as if he'd just strolled from Tattersalls after a winning streak. Were they here to spy on us or 'psyche' us out? No, no . . . he came bearing gifts.

There were stickers for our car: long blue things saying '*Country Life* Record Bird Watch' which, had we put them on our windscreen, would have totally obliterated our view of the road. Their ruse didn't work. We cut off the '*Country Life*' bit and replaced it with a discreet and tiny *ffPS* emblem. David also offered 'Moet & Chandon Champagne' stickers, 'because they're backing us both' and had donated six huge bottles as prizes in the raffle. Be that as it doubtless was . . . our gratitude was tainted a little by the fact that David had already sold all the tickets to his friends. (This isn't entirely true. I heard later that Cyril Walker had managed to buy a ticket on the black market. He didn't win, despite the fact that I drew the raffle.)

David also brought us a nice set of forms for us to fill in with our birds, and a plastic folder containing a new set of rules. I don't know why, but it all seemed strangely intimidating. Maybe that was why Cliff attempted a bit of gamesmanship. We knew they must have seen the RAF vehicle parked outside and may well have been musing whether or not we had air transport. Bill Urwin was casually invited over to exchange pleasantries, before which Cliff flipped the British Isles Atlas open at . . . Central Scotland. Bill's eyes certainly registered the page, though he said nothing. To increase suspicion Cliff 'surreptitiously' closed the book before Bill could take a second glance. *Country Life* bid us a cheery farewell and good luck and left us feeling that there was at least a sporting chance that they believed we'd lined up an RAF jump-jet to whip us up to the Cairngorms to tick off Capercaillie. Certainly just before David T. vaulted into his Porsche he quipped: 'I hope the helicopter doesn't crash.' Had they fallen for our mischievous little prank? I forgot to ask! Actually if they *did*, it may have been our big mistake – it probably gave them the added incentive to try and murder us!!

We were left to enjoy the nicely typed new rules . . . some of which really were new. The new lateness rule: 'For every one minute after midnight, 10 minutes will be counted back and any bird seen during that period will be deleted'. Mm . . . let's see . . . 1982 . . . they had Stone Curlew at 22.46 and they were 9 minutes late . . . so that's 9 × 10 . . . 90 minutes . . . half past ten. See . . . we DID draw!

Next rule: 'A list of birds recorded must be placed before the judge on the stroke of midnight.' Otherwise we turn into pumpkins?

'Records of rarities must be accepted by the Rarities Committee.' Does that mean if we see a rarity we have to wait nine months for the committee to consider the record before we know who's won? Wait a minute . . . Tim Inskipp's *on* the Rarities Committee . . . let's hope *Country Life* claim a rarity. Actually three years ago on their first record run they claimed a Caspian Tern which was eventually rejected, probably on the grounds of 'facetiousness'. As Tim recalled, David T. described it as 'smaller than a passing yacht'. Or was it 'bigger'? Anyway, they'd be well advised to stick to common birds.

Another new rule increased our suspicion of the Moet stickers: 'A magnum of champagne will be awarded to the winning team. (It is not essential either to share it with the beaten opponents or to drink it at midnight.)'

'Beaten opponents' . . . I suppose that meant us. At least it didn't say 'losers'!

At 18.00, with a parting plea – 'everyone look out for Whinchats' – our meeting broke up and our team leapt into the Land Rover for a little run to remind us what birdwatching was like. Within half an hour we'd ticked

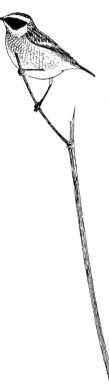

ffPS

Cock Whinchat

off both species of godwit and Whimbrel – all birds that were to take us over half a day on the race!

At 19.30 on Friday I left John and Cliff ambling off for 'no more than one pint' at the White Hart. Tim, his wife Carol, myself, and my girl friend Laura, returned to John Burton's for an excellent supper prepared by John's wife, Viv. With amazing discipline I went to bed at 21.30 and fell asleep lulled by the soothing squeals of Burton's pet Barn Owl which was flitting round its enclosure in the back garden.

I awoke before the alarm, expecting it to be about 10.00. It was 01.25 on Saturday morning. Time to get up. I got dressed, kissed Laura farewell and fell down the stairs. As I brushed my teeth I had difficulty focussing on my face in the mirror – a blessing at the time. No doubt my eyes would open fully by the time I needed to use binoculars. I sat and waited for Tim to get up, mulling over a few thoughts on the day ahead. 'It sounds dry and calm out there' ... 'Nice to have all this back-up ... but in a way it's a pity ... I hope we find some stuff for ourselves.' ... 'Ah ... 'morning Tim ... ready?'

As we drove the 3 or 4 miles to Cliff's cottage several cars passed us. I was convinced every one was a *Country Life* back-up vehicle. I had to remind myself that 01.45 was not an outrageous time for Friday night revellers to be going home. They probably assumed we were going home too ... how silly. Of course we were going ... birdwatching! At 2.00 we arrived at Angel Cottage. John and Cliff were up and ready.

The account that follows is my own. The rest of my team may have seen it a different way, or indeed have more accurate memories. I recorded my thoughts on a small tape-recorder which worked pretty well, while Tim recorded our birds on another one which often didn't. Since I fled to Shetland the minute the race was over I have seen neither Tim's official timings nor been able to consult on the facts. So this account is mine – a sort of diary as it happened, rather than looking back on it. I don't remember the names of all the places we went, and in fact I *never* knew some of them. I've even forgotten some of the particularly immemorable birds ... I've no idea when we first heard a House Sparrow, and I don't recall seeing a Jackdaw – but we did, honestly!

So here it goes then: the *ffPS* account of the 'Big Bird Race 1983' . . .

02.00. Already I've no idea what's going on. Contrary to tradition, we're *not* starting in Cliff's old Land Rover. Or rather *I'm* not. Tim and Cliff *are*. John and I follow them in the Saab. At 02.10 we are led down a muddy path into the woods and stop outside a small wooden hut. What's in here? – a Barn Owl perhaps? Cliff leaps out, dives into the hut, and emerges carrying . . . a pair of welly-boots. Apparently Tim has forgotten to bring his wellies and so we've dropped in at a secret welly-boot-hut known only to Cliff. I get the feeling that Cliff is so well organised that he's planted spare wellies all along the route. As Tim changes footwear, we hear our first bird: 02.10 Nightingale. There's a spray of rain in the air – worrying; or perhaps it'll bring down some migrants, though frankly the wind is not promising, barely east of south, in fact maybe due south . . . or, be honest, it's still south-west. We leave the Saab by the hut and all get into the Land Rover. I'm sitting in the front with John – an incredible treat for me – being in the front, that is (though it's very nice to be with John too). Tim is in the back – the stillness of the night is disrupted only by his yells of agony. I sympathise. I was in the back for the past two years. There are no seats and no cushions, just lots of iron things and a couple of telescopes scattered around waiting to be fallen on. Cliff drives over ruts and bumps that would defeat a Centurion tank. Whoever's in the back is either flung upward, cracking his head on the roof, or downwards shattering his bum on an iron thing. If he grabs onto the back door handle it flies open, and he falls out. The pain takes longer to describe than to experience. It's now 02.12, we are hurtling along a smoother bit of lane (i.e. the potholes are only a foot deep) when we see car lights some way behind us. We are convinced it's a *Country Life* back-up vehicle. Perhaps their plan is to follow us all night and let us lead them to the birds.

At the moment we're heading for a Long-eared Owl site that they may not know of. Cliff accelerates and Tim nearly flies out of the back. We turn off our lights and swing off into an invisible field. The car behind continues on the main track and fades into the night.

Nightingale

It's like something out of 'Minder'! 02.15. We're out on foot stumbling behind Cliff in pitch darkness. Every now and then car lights blink in the distance. We feel certain we are surrounded by *Country Life* back-up people. I expect they're hiding behind every tree. (I haven't felt like this since I went for a stroll on Hampstead Heath late on a Saturday Night . . . and discovered that most of the silver birches were young men in white leather trousers! Fortunately I was with Laura at the time.) Maybe we're a little paranoid. Suddenly Cliff whispers: 'Look – they're signalling to each other with a flashlight!' John corrects him: 'That's a lighthouse' . . . It is, and we are – paranoid, that is. 02.30 and we're still trying for Long-eared Owl. Cliff is doing a very believable impersonation. Not good enough to convince the owl but I *am* worried that *Country Life* might hear it and tick it off! A Tawny Owl is impressed too and replies – or maybe he wasn't so impressed: it was *meant* to be a Long-eared.

We decide we'll try again later and go and try for Savi's Warbler instead. As we creep back to the car both Tim and I are having tape-recorder trouble. Tim's little Talk-book keeps whining instead of talking. Feed-back? I eventually realise it's telling us the tape is in the wrong way. I keep pressing 'play' instead of 'record'! Unfortunately I'm using an old tape. A quick burst of a rock-and-roll version of 'Swan Lake' blasts through the night! At least it's appropriate.

02.40. We're parked nearer the marsh now. It's surprising perhaps how many of these 'reedy' warblers sing at night. Sedge Warbler rattling away. Grasshopper Warbler reeling – one of our *last* birds last year. Nice to have got it so early. Reed Warbler. The expected squeaks, squeals and quacks of Moorhen, Lapwing and Mallard. A Redshank yelps. It always feels encouraging to get so much in the dead of night before the day really even begins; but it's a false optimism – most of these birds would be easy at any time. The point is – for now – no Savi's Warbler reeling. So that's two unsuccessful 'sites' already and nearly an hour gone.

It's a weird feeling racing around in the dark high on adrenalin – a sort of blind stage-fright. I wonder if Stevie Wonder feels like this before a show?

Cliff jogs back to the Land Rover – something the rest of us don't risk as we don't know where our feet are.

We rattle back to the Long-eared Owl area. The theory is that though *Country Life* may well cover the same terrain *we*, or rather the Rover, can drive most of the way. The Porsche will have to park on the main road and they'll have to walk further than us. One fact is, of course, they'll probably run, or their back-up team will carry them, or they may well have a bulldozer. Really we're trying to convince ourselves that our slow start is not too disastrous. A Black-headed Gull calls.

We decide to split into pairs to listen for the owl. This is of course dangerous. It's all too easy for two people to hear a single call and the other two to miss it. It happened to us last year with a nocturnal Golden Plover – I always claimed our score was 152-and-a-half.

Cliff is doing his Long-eared impersonation again – it's *just* inaccurate enough not to confuse me and John. The thought strikes me: it says in the rules that 'tape-recorders must not be used to attract or stimulate birds'. Why not? If you allow walky-talkies, back-up teams, helicopters and impersonations – why not tape-recorders? Anyway, just after 03.00 . . . John and I sort of sense that Cliff is gesticulating to us from about 200 yards away. We scamper up to him. He does *his* owl and a Long-eared Owl answers. There's a subtle difference between the calls: I thought Cliff's was better. This really is a thrilling moment – so dark, so quiet and with no-one else 'marking' the bird for us. Or . . . is it the *Country Life* team making owl noises!? answering Cliff . . . or is Cliff answering them? Cliff calls again – the owl replies – actually it *is* a better Long-eared than Cliff's. '03.something . . . Long-eared Owl' – as I record the event I accidentally hit the 'play' button and a rock-and-roll fanfare celebrates the achievement.

03.20 and we are heading back into the Land Rover. It's amazing how morale goes up and down. I was just thinking 'what a bad start' – then the owl calls and we're 'up' again. John points out the advantage of the early start. Maybe we went to slightly the wrong sites first but it's still only 03.20. Last year we were just getting up! Actually it's 03.30 as we swap vehicles. Out of the Rover and into the Saab. The purr of the Turbo engine is drowned by a Cetti's Warbler, and another burst from my recorder rouses a cross captive Peacock from a nearby ornamental garden. Alas Peacock doesn't count – or maybe it will in the event of a draw?

Time 03.00

10 species

Long-eared Owl

Time 04.00

20 species

Next journey, a slightly irritating detour. There have been no Bitterns booming at Walberswick this year and obviously it would be a ridiculous irony to dip out on what I suppose is almost East Anglia's 'National Bird' as it were. So we're driving to Dunwich Cliffs in a heavy rainstorm. What if *this* goes on all day? That could change a few plans! It *might* even suit us, as Cliff has several places we can drive to and stay in the Land Rover using it as a hide. But then there are lots of real hides *Country Life* can use and keep dry in . . . 'Boooom!' 04.00-ish . . . Bittern . . . Back in the Saab . . . We are now heading down back lanes to a farm near which *should* be Little Owls. This is a sensitive bird for us. We missed it last year although we had several 'sites'. We've always rather felt that we could have had Little Owl as our last bird on the Saturday night if we'd risked being a few minutes late. We'd chosen not to, since the rule stated 'back at midnight'. I think we can be allowed a little wince at the fact that *Country Life* then turned up at '24.09', or later (depending which watch you looked at) . . . Anyway . . . it's all in fun, isn't it . . .? Where's that bloody Little Owl?

We park and splash through a farmyard. The farm dog barks violently, a sound that always panics me. I hurry ahead. Already it's getting light and I'm fretting that we are not going to be in the right place for those birds which only appear or call at dawn and dusk. Or maybe *this* is the right place. A Skylark starts singing . . . a Snipe starts drumming . . . and, best of all, a Wood-cock croaks as it buzzes a nearby wood. Last year we struggled for Snipe and missed Woodcock. No Little Owl yet, but two good birds . . .

04.14 . . . and the dawn chorus is beginning to accelerate. This is not really where we'd choose to be at this time . . . but does it really matter? The sky is grey and it's raining on and off. It's not going to be a great dawn chorus and if the sun comes out later the birds may well try again and have a second burst. The point is: there are a number of woodland species that are a lot easier to hear than see and especially during the first moments of daylight; we might waste a lot of time searching for them later in the day. The problem is: there are several places we'd like to be at dawn – in the woods, back at the marsh . . . or here? I console myself with the Woodcock as we wade through wet grass and acquire soggy trousers. Suddenly a Little Owl takes pity and calls loud and clear from a nearby tree. Back to the car with more 'common birds' starting up – Song Thrush, Red-legged Partridge and a Cuckoo, not only cuckooing but also giving that lovely effervescent bubbling call – must be a pair; I suppose they must get together sometime!

04.20-ish . . . We're now racing back to the marshes to make sure we have another go at Savi's Warbler before it gets too light and maybe too late. I keep muttering that I have heard them singing in the mid-afternoon in Kent, but apparently the Suffolk birds are shyer. It's not like the *ffPS* team to go anywhere in a straight line . . . and we don't. We decide to have a quick bash at Barn Owl – always a dodgy bird on race-days. Two years ago, on the eve of the 1981 race, I drove all the way back to John Burton's with a Barn Owl flying parallel along the roadside hedge. The next day it was the last bird we had and then only a brief call. Ironically this area of Suffolk is one of the best places in England for simply 'bumping into' Barn Owls. Right now we're stopping by a lane down which one of Cliff's friends jogs most mornings accompanied by a Barn Owl. Maybe it comes out to have a laugh. We try jogging. It doesn't work and the first Chaffinch of the day is hardly a consolation.

04.41. Another hopeful Barn Owl spot. Here it's a row of trees in which the owls often snooze during day-light hours. Ironically it's probably still too dark for them – they're probably away hunting. A Blue Tit calls – that's no consolation either, neither is a Great Tit, nor a distant Pheasant.

04.45 and we're on our way back to Cliff's cottage. We stop at the corner of the saltings to scan for Short-eared Owl which are often quartering the marshes in the early light. And now it *is* light – and for the first time we can use binoculars and see, as well as hear, our birds. A Rook flies over; not surprising as there's a huge rookery visible by the roadside. Swallows; and Jackdaws – at least that's what my tape-recorder tells me. Starlings and a pair of Mute Swans. Then one of those unexpected bonuses that can make the day. John suddenly yells 'Garganey'. At that moment we were all looking in different directions but as if drawn by the Garganey's magnetic force we all whip round in time

Cuckoo

30 species

to see it – a female – flying fast away from us down a dyke. Five seconds later it was gone. It would have been so easy for at least one of us to have missed it. Another good bird – last year we used up half the morning searching the marshes for Garganey. 04.51 and we pile back in the Land Rover and mull over the morning so far. Some you win . . . Woodcock, Little Owl, Snipe, Grasshopper Warbler and Garganey, all of which proved difficult last year . . . but we still haven't got Barn or Short-eared Owl.

04.58. Back at the Cottage now to pick up the Saab and our walky-talky which we'd forgotten along with Tim's wellies. We have a go. 'Corn Bunting to Grouse'. Silence. We had arranged to call our back-up team at 04.00, though none of us can think why. Maybe it was meant to be their alarm call. John tries again 'Come in Grouse'. If we do get through we'll say 'we're at the cottage – just about to set off !' – three hours late! Our naughty ruse is scuppered – we can't get through. 05.00.

Both vehicles are on the move making an *ffPS* bee-line for Savi's Warbler, which means we'll stop at least six times on the way. First detour – Stone Curlew. This should be easy. Cliff has discovered a pair nesting in an open field right by the road. We arrive and park. Wait a minute, is this the right field? It doesn't look quite the same as a couple of days ago. It *is* the right field but it's *not* the same – the farmer has been over it with the seed drilling machine! Understandably the Stone Curlews have quit their nest. John and Cliff curse the fact that they didn't bother to check the site yesterday, while a Whitethroat, a Willow Warbler, and a couple of Turtle Doves attempt to cheer us up. I record them at 05.04

while Cliff tries to figure out where he would go if he was a Stone Curlew who'd just been drilled off its eggs. He has a theory, and at about 05.15 we are wandering around at a crossroads about a mile away. As we're wondering which way to try, we get directions: 'Curleeeee' – a distant Stone Curlew points the way, only now that we've heard it we don't need to go. Instead, I indicate a passing Bullfinch which unfortunately passes so quickly that Cliff doesn't see it.

05.20, and the same sort of thing happens again. We've dropped the Saab again and are all back in the Land Rover. I'm back in the back and Tim's back in the front, from where he sees – a Great Spotted Woodpecker – alas, it was 'spotted' only by Tim. We all leap out and scamper around, but the bird goes on the 'irritation list' along with the Bullfinch. At 05.21 'Corn Bunting' makes contact with 'Famous Grouse', who inform us that they are waiting for us at their headquarters, a cottage deep in the Fenland woods about half a mile away. The implication is that the walkytalky's range is about half a mile . . . almost shouting distance! 'Corn Bunting' informs 'Grouse' that we are hell bent on Savi's Warbler, at which point we stop and get out again as we happen to be passing a good Tree Pipit spot. These little stops are not as frustrating as might be feared, as we invariably pick up new birds at this early stage. 05.22 Blackcap. 05.25 Mistle Thrush, 05.32 Green Woodpecker and 05.35, as intended, Tree Pipit. A pause for a resumé. It's 05.35, really pretty late; *Country Life* are usually getting near their century by now! We have no idea how many we've seen, but it's nowhere near that. We've probably missed Barn Owl and maybe Short-eared and we still haven't had a concentrated period in the woods picking up those relatively common birds that can so easily get forgotten – Long-tailed Tit, Coal Tit, Redstart, Tree Sparrow, Lesser Whitethroat and so on. We never actually set out to see any of them at any particular place but rather assume we will have simply come across them somewhere by the end of the day. But maybe we won't . . . maybe there'll be something really silly we sort of 'forget to see'. It always bothers me – after all a Savi's Warbler is worth no more than a Linnet!

05.35, Linnet.

05.37, Canada Goose calling as we stop again, this time at a site that really has to be visited. We draw up quietly by the nest-hole of a Lesser Spotted Woodpecker. It's all very well finding the nest but of course Lesser Spotteds can sit in there for half the day without peeping out or making a sound. This one has a greater sense of responsibility. No doubt aware that we 'need it' quickly, it appears in the branches behind the nesthole, not only earning its sponsorship money but reminding us how rarely one gets a really good view of a Lesser Spot. Alas, we have no time to enjoy it. Back in the Land Rover we count up our woodpeckers – Green, Lesser Spotted and a quarter of a Great Spotted . . . we

Green
Woodpecker

50 species

might regret that one. But no. Bang on cue, the three in the front yell 'Great Spotted'. I yell . . . 'Where?!' 'Outside the car'. I didn't think it was *inside*! 'Bill – can you see it?' In a misplaced fit of confidence and not wishing to upset the other three I answer 'yes', and then focus on a passing Starling. 'That's not it.' 'It's still with us' yells Cliff and slows down to allow the bird to catch up. For the next 50 yards it flies ahead of us down the lane until we have to 'beep' it to move out of the way. All three woodpeckers – always a nice set.

05.44. At last we stop by the marsh for our second attempt at Savi's Warbler – a bird we'd hoped to have got three hours ago. As we walk down, the score continues to mount: Swift, Garden Warbler singing; Coot calling. Cliff scuttles on ahead of us and crouches behind a clay bank that forms a screen between bird-watchers and one of the small pools on the reserve. He peeps through the shutters of the one-man hide and beckons us to see Teal, Gadwall, and ironically, in view of our earlier luck, another Garganey – this time a superb male. Tim, John and I have no eyes for ducks yet though, as our relieved ears are happily tuning in to the welcome reeling of a Savi's Warbler. I walk on to join Cliff . . . 'Savi's – O.K.?' . . . 'No!.' 'But Listen,

View from high ground of a male Marsh Harrier quartering the reed-beds in its hunt for prey

it's singing all the time.' Cliff and I listen – nothing. Surely it's not going to stop now!? 'It *is* getting late' Cliff reminds me. 'Yes but it was singing ten seconds ago.' We look back to John and Tim only 50 yards away. They give a thumbs-up and point at the marsh. We listen again – nothing. What *is* going on? 'We were hearing it all the way coming down . . . ah . . . hang on.' Cliff and I set off back up the hill. No sooner are we out of the lea of the bank than the breeze carries the sound to us as clear as . . . as clear as a Savi's Warbler.

All four of us squeeze into the one-man hide to enjoy the Garganey and tick off the Teal, Gadwall, and Common Tern. For the next half hour we walked along the back of the marshes adding birds all the way. 05.50 Reed Bunting . . . 05.54 Grey Heron . . . 05.55 half a Long-tailed Tit – Cliff and I dip out! . . . 06.00 Marsh Harrier, a fine male . . . and Greylag Goose . . . 06.03 the other half of the Long-tailed Tit . . . Goldcrest . . . 06.18 Jay . . . 06.20 Stock Dove.

At 06.22 we are climbing the ladders of the tall 'tower' hide that gives a panoramic view over the marshes. This is the area that has provided the bulk of our early birds in previous years. Today, because we were out so early, we've got most of these. We're mainly

60 species

Time 06.00

70 species

hoping for Water Rail – a bird far more often heard than seen. As if to prove it Cliff and I hear one squeaking on our side of the hide. Tim and John, on the other side, don't hear it. 06.26, a Pied Wagtail flits in front of the hide. This is often a good place to get a Sparrowhawk gliding from one wood to another, but it's such a chancy event we're not going to wait for long. A couple of minutes later the noise of us giving up disturbs the Water Rail again and everyone hears it.

06.30. That's about it for the marshes. We return to where the vehicles are parked by a small wood near a farm house with a scrubby garden and some nice telegraph wires and fence posts for flycatchers and chats. The sun is coming out now and the wind is dropping. This may well be a good place to listen for that 'second dawn-chorus'. Last year we did rather well here, with Nuthatch, Treecreeper, Lesser Whitethroat and Tree Sparrow all in a matter of moments. Already today there's a Spotted Flycatcher on the wires. So at 06.34 we settle down for a quick listen . . . it doesn't take long. A screech of brakes behind us and

one of Cliff's assistants tumbles out of a car. 'Short-eared Owl sitting on a post.' 'Is it still there?' Why do birders always ask that question? Knowing full well a bird can fly off the minute your back's turned! Our helper is patient; no doubt he appreciates the strain we are under . . . 'Well it was still there when I left it ten minutes ago.' 'Where where?'

A minute went by as we tried to coincide points of reference then someone had a better idea. We *all* (helper included) got back into the Land Rover and careered off down more tracks that were definitely 'unsuitable for motor vehicles'. After 6 minutes – it took the car 10! – we emerged on to a hill overlooking the caravan site at Walberswick.

At least half a mile away we could see a lump of mud sitting on a post. Kim set up his telescope and re-identified the lump. 06.41, Short-eared Owl. It's not often either team gets all the owls – four down, one to go.

At 06.00 we'd supposedly settled down for that listen in the woods. With typical *ffPS* waywardness it was

ffPS

BILL ODDIE

By the ruined mill near Walberswick, a Short-eared Owl searches the reeds for prey.

over an hour before we were to return. It was as if the Short-eared Owl had been a sign that we ought to go rambling again; so we did. 06.44, we're surveying a disused football pitch which recently supported a Fieldfare. Today it sports 2 Blackbirds, 3 Mistle Thrushes, a man and a dog. A Redpoll flies over trilling gaily – that's another species we sort of assume we'll see sometime but just might not. There are also Herring Gulls on the horizon. Surely we've seen *them* before now? but if we have, we haven't recorded the fact. 06.46, a Wheatear flies across in front of the Land Rover. We're still heading away from the woods so, as Cliff puts it, we 'might as well' go and have a look at one of his flood pools by the Blyth estuary.

80 species

06.50, we add Shoveler and Meadow Pipit, and a Spotted Redshank calls as it disappears over the sea-wall. Now that *is* a good one to get, there's not a lot about. In fact we don't see another one all day. There's also a Common Sandpiper, and, behind us, our temporary fifth team member points out a male Yellow Wagtail sitting on a post. I presume we would have noticed it eventually, but I suppose this proves that five pairs of eyes are better than four. Then again, where do you draw the line? – twenty pairs are no doubt better than five, but doesn't it sort of make a nonsense of the team-of-four idea? 06.54, Kestrel hovering way in the distance. Tim spots it. No help required.

Now we've come this far we 'might as well' have a look at the estuary itself. The tide is low and on most average days in May we could reasonably expect to see Grey Plover, Whimbrel, Greenshank and godwits. In fact the only visible waders are a party of three 'little ones' tazzing away from us as if they felt they were spoiling the purity of the empty view. 06.55, two Dunlin and a Ringed Plover. The only other new bird is Great Black-backed Gull. News from Minsmere was 'few waders' and the same from Norfolk. Blythburgh confirms it.

Time 07.00

It is now 07.00 and I'm still fretting about 'little birds'. I really do feel we should be getting back to the woods. We turn round and head back, adding Stone-chat through the window at 07.04. This is a good 'incidental bird' and has saved us a special trip to Westleton Heath. Even better, two minutes later a pair of Grey Partridges scamper across the track almost under our bonnet. This is one time that I in the back spot the birds first, probably because the bonnet is about as far as I can see. The others are understandably looking at the road ahead as the partridges try to slip under their gaze. Fortunately they stop to watch us go by, and *we* watch *them*. Another useful species, as Greys are outnumbered by Red-leggeds several to one in these parts, and last year we didn't see any till after tea-time. 07.08, Goldfinches fly past the windscreen and at 07.15 we arrive back at the little wood to continue our 06.00 listen. One advantage of not having a rigid schedule is that you don't really feel you're behind it, until you've really screwed everything up. At the moment we feel 'flexible' rather than 'screwed up'.

The weather is now sunny and fairly calm and I'm hopeful birds will be singing in appreciation, and that this spot will prove as productive as last year. It would be nice to get Tree Sparrow here, and Redstart. 07.20, a Redstart sings as we're making sure everyone sees a Coal Tit which is swinging tantalisingly through the trees above us. Then a Nuthatch calls, and next a Bullfinch, which Cliff needs to add to the three quarters we had a couple of hours back. So far . . . pretty good. We give it a few more minutes, searching for Tree Sparrow and Lesser Whitethroat before nervously relegating them to 'birds we assume we'll pick up later'. How late we didn't then know!

It is now about 07.30. It feels as if it's the end of the 'first phase' as it were. We haven't been keeping a running total and Tim hasn't been filling in his form as it was clearly designed to be written on in a Porsche not a Land Rover. We have no idea what our score is. Cliff reckons it must be over the hundred. I reckon it's well short. (In fact it was 93.) We now return to Fen Cottage to indulge in some proper communication with our back-up forces. Fen Cottage nestles deep in the forest, looking rather like a dilapidated ginger-bread house from some fairy tale or Christmas panto. Our back-up cast look as if they're already in costume for the same panto. There are 'woodsmen' in lumberjack shirts; little chaps in scarlet hoods as worn by gnomes and dwarves; men in Lincoln green; even two strapping blond 'principal boys' in jolly hats with gaily coloured artificial parrots on them. The three bears were presumably still inside enjoying their breakfast, which

Cock Stonechat

90 species

smelled more like bacon than porridge. The principal boys with parrots on their heads turned out to be two girls from the staff of the British Museum where Cyril Walker works. I'm sure they had no idea what they'd let themselves in for. The idea of helping on a 'Big Bird Race' probably sounds like a right old romp until you do it. After you've sat at a defunct Woodlark site for four hours with a duff walky-talky waiting for a team who never turn up it must lose a little of the glamour.

Meanwhile at 07.30 the parrots look fresh and perky and cheer us up no end. Identifiable figures emerge from the merry throng: John Burton, Tim Parmenter and Mark Carwardine, all of whom have already been out in the surrounding woods and give us useful news, though some of it is negative. 'Is the Wood Warbler singing behind the cottage as it was yesterday?' 'No.' It isn't that we distrust the information, but we immediately dive into the forest to have a listen. Sure enough, there's no Wood Warbler. Our back-up team is obviously working well. As if to confirm it, they inform us that they haven't found any Woodlarks either. We immediately race to the nearby Woodlark site, not because we don't believe them but because they *have* seen a couple of Crossbills where the Woodlarks should be, but aren't. There aren't any Crossbills either but it's worth a wait. We'd sort of crossed Crossbills off, if you'll pardon the expression, as Cliff reckoned the recent wet weather had provided them with such a prolific choice of drinking pools that it is pretty nigh impossible to predict their appearance at any particular spot. They might just fly over and call, but how long do we wait for this possible unexpected bonus? We decide to give it ten minutes, hoping in our hearts that our back-up boys might be wrong about the Woodlarks as well. Alas, they *are* entirely reliable. No Woodlarks and no Crossbills either. At 07.43 we move on, leaving the non-involved John Burton to sit there for the next four hours in case the Crossbills come back.

We follow Tim Parmenter to another part of the same forest where half an hour before he'd come across a pair of Willow Tits, another notoriously difficult localised species. 'How are you doing?' he enquires. 'Not great – we haven't even heard a Chiffchaff yet.' Apparently we only needed to ask. 07.45, Chiffchaff singing. We are now at the Willow Tit spot – it looks pretty unlikely – a tall dry conifer forest with only a few sparse bushes as lower foliage. For five minutes we wander around, feeling Crossbill is more likely. Then Cliff spots a rotten tree stump with a couple of old holes in the top . . . 'Now if I were a Willow Tit . . .' The bird itself pops its head out and agrees. 07.48, Willow Tit. Thank you, back-up. We drive back to Fen Cottage where the invisible Wood Warbler is still refusing to sing. We can see the RAF team and Cyril – collectively 'Dipper' – passing round the walky-talky and taking it in turns to call 'Corn Bunting'. We should be able to hear them, and indeed we can, but this is because we're only ten yards away. John decides to test the system 'Corn Bunting calling'. For the tenth time already this morning the three of us whip round anxiously 'Where?' They should have called us 'Wood Warbler' and *really* upset us! The RAF team are pretending they can't hear John's natural voice while admitting they certainly can't hear him over the walky-talky. 'Corn Bunting' and 'Dipper' advance ever closer to each other till their noses (or should it be beaks?) are almost touching. Suddenly distorted electronic voices replace the acoustic sound 'Come in Dipper.' 'Over.' 'Dipper receiving Corn Bunting; are you hearing *me*?' 'Hearing you loud and clear.' So they should be! Personally I'm not greatly impressed that our communication link has an effective range of two inches. The RAF man convincingly argues that the walky-talkies are more effective than we think; otherwise Britain's military powers wouldn't rely on them. 'Early warning! Russian missile at two inches . . . ouch! Too late.' . . . I believe him. There's a quick lecture on pressing the right buttons, and a change of batteries, and we agree we'll do a proper test once we're on the move again, which we should be now.

08.00. We call back at Angel Cottage to leave the Saab and carry on in the Land Rover. In previous years we would no doubt have been tempted by the possibility of a cooked breakfast. This year we content ourselves with pinching bits of Robbie's bacon and eggs which she was no doubt looking forward to immensely. Mark Carwardine has been sent off to north Norfolk and will be waiting with news when we arrive, probably about 15.00 or 16.00. 'Dipper' is off to

Time 08.00

Marsh Tit (*above*)
and Willow Tit

Benacre to see what's there – we should join him in about an hour from now. I'm not sure where 'Sun Grebe' is; and 'Grouse' is stuck in the woods waiting for Crossbills, no doubt beginning to think his call-sign is rather appropriate. *We* are off to 'the Hawfinch wood', a site which remains nameless both in the interests of the bird's privacy and because I have no idea what it was called or where it was. We're all in the Land Rover and Cliff is driving; I just sit in the back and do as I'm told. On the way, 'Corn Bunting' and 'Dipper' exchange some snappy radio jargon and establish that if you press the right buttons, put in new batteries, and leave the contraptions switched on, the walky-talkies have an effective range of nearly two miles – a lot better than two inches. Definitely worth having.

08.05. We have parked the Land Rover and are strolling through a really delightful wood. Last year – one compares everything with 'last year'! – a pair of Hawfinches flew over the moment we arrived. This year we're having to walk . . . and walk. There are still 'incidentals' to be picked up and we do: 08.11, Marsh Tit . . . Marsh *and* Willow Tit, that's one of the pairs that sort of imply you're doing well – like getting all the woodpeckers, which we have – or all the owls, which we haven't . . . yet. 08.19, Treecreeper. Fine . . . but it's getting late . . . not only for us, but maybe also for the Hawfinches. On recent mornings, Cliff has been hearing them regularly up to about 07.30 but after that they tend to be more elusive. It's now nearly 08.30. We split up – always a potentially risky move – and within five minutes the point is proved. Tim hears a single call and sets off after it . . . I don't know whether to follow him or go and get John and Cliff, neither of whom are even visible. I spot John and shout to him, risking frightening the Hawfinches – O.K. they might call as they fly off, but would Cliff hear them? He can't even hear *me*. I'm concerned that Hawfinch might become an obsession for Cliff. Its understandable: this is sort of 'his wood' and he knows the birds are here and are usually quick and easy – something one can rarely say of such a notoriously secretive species. There's a temptation to wait for them no matter how long it takes. The same thing happened a bit with Garganey last year. We wandered round the fens for an hour in the early morning searching for a Garganey that was definitely there somewhere. We saw neither it nor anything else. If we dip out on Hawfinch now, we probably won't get it later in the day and it'll certainly be a blow to morale. On the other hand, we have to remind ourselves that a Hawfinch is worth no more than a Tree Sparrow or a Lesser Whitethroat, neither of which we've had yet. I was hoping for *them* in this wood too. Cliff is no doubt having similar thoughts. He re-appears and, surprisingly cheerily, admits 'we'd better get on'.

I sometimes think birds have consciences. No sooner had we regrouped and headed back in the direction of the Land Rover than an unseen but noisy family of Hawfinches 'tsipped' us farewell from a nearby hornbeam. 08.39 . . . last year two minutes, this year over half an hour. Still, it took me twenty five *years* to see my first Hawfinch!

100 species

08.52, and yet again we're back at Angel Cottage. In previous years this is the sort of time we'd be off down to Minsmere. This year we're off *up* to Benacre. The logistics are almost complex. We are to take both Saab and Land Rover to Benacre plus an extra driver. The team will then use the Rover to cover some of the rougher ground. We will then rejoin the Saab and drive in that to Lowestoft, whilst the extra driver takes the Land Rover, refuels it, and returns it to the cottage so we can use it later for a final fling round various flood pools. This degree of efficiency is quite contrary to *ffPS* tradition. We don't exactly have a time-schedule, but we have a rough idea of where we'd like to be and when. We'd hope to be away from Suffolk and on our way to north Norfolk by not much after 13.00, with a total of something like 140 birds. Before then we have to do Benacre, Lowestoft, Minsmere and a few bits in between. Meanwhile we still haven't added up our score at 09.15 as we arrive in the area of Benacre. 'Recent Reports and News' over the past days has been good from here: Kentish Plover, Sanderling, Mediterranean and Little Gulls, and there should be duck on gravel pits and waders on the Broad. Benacre takes a little time to 'do', but it should be worth it.

Time 09.00

The pits are in fact disappointing. Common Gull, Little Tern and a couple of Pochard flying past. I'm sure we were all hoping for a 'bonus' or two here . . .

105 species

maybe a Red-breasted Merganser, or a migrant Whinchat on the nearby bushes. At half past nine we stop
and have a quick 'sea-watch'. Not a lot moving . . .
maybe we're a bit late in the day. It's that old problem
– how many places can you be at the same time? There's
no doubt sea-watching on this coast, especially when
the wind isn't even blowing onshore, is not likely to be
very productive except in the early hours. But then
that's also the time to be in the woods, or down at the
marsh or . . . never mind . . . let's have a look at the
Broad. As we approach Benacre Broad it 'looks' good
. . . the water is low, and there's lots of nice muddy
shoreline and shingly banks. It just looks like a place
for rare birds. I've a feeling Benacre will probably have
some really good days this spring . . . but not today.

110 species

There are two new waders: 09.38, Greenshank and
Turnstone; and there's other new birds as well: Little
Grebe, Tufted Duck and a bunch of Kittiwakes on the
shingle. But where's the Sanderling and the Kentish
Plover and . . . and where's 'Dipper'?

The RAF vehicle had left for Benacre ages ago and
they were supposed to be meeting us. They *must* be
less than two miles away. 'Corn Bunting' to 'Dipper'
. . . come in 'Dipper' . . . come in 'Sun Grebe' . . .
'Grouse' . . . 'Starship Enterprise' . . . anybody!!! Across

the other side of the Broad we spot a windblown figure in a bright blue anorak carrying a telecope on a tripod. A quick squint through our binoculars reveals he's also carrying a walky-talky. 'Corn Bunting to Dipper' . . . 'Dipper can you hear me?' . . . 'Switch the bloody thing on!' Cyril couldn't hear, but he could see, so he waved, and we waved back, and then mimed for him to switch on his walky-talky, or, better still, keep moving and meet us on the beach at the corner of the broad.

09.55, Cyril gives us the kind of news every team wants to hear. 'You should have been here an hour ago. Lots of stuff moving at sea . . . Merganser, Gannets, Common and Velvet Scoter.' Out of that lot, Common Scoter is about the only one we feel fairly confident of getting later. As we feared – we *are* too late for the sea-watch. We decide to keep trying though . . . the team watches the Broad whilst Cyril watches the sea. 09.58, the gulls scatter and the terns start screeching . . . there must be a raptor around. I'm the first to spot it – its flying away from us – the worst view possible – tail end and getting smaller. Fortunately, the mobbing terns guide everyone's eyes and the bird finally swoops and rolls into the safety of the woods giving away its identity: Sparrowhawk. Definitely a good one to get.

A hunting Sparrowhawk hurtles low along the edge of Benacre Broad.

Time 10.00

Amongst the panicking gulls was a Lesser Black-back, the first of the day, and behind us at 10.06 a Sandwich Tern patrols the beach.

It was about now that another major frustration occurs. Around ten o'clock Cliff was scanning the distant horizon over the woodlands when a flurry of crows rose from the tree tops looking almost as indignant as the gulls and terns had done. Is it another Sparrow-hawk . . . or something bigger? The light isn't good at this time – it's getting rather grey and blustery – but Cliff is convinced that he'd caught a glimpse of a large raptor being harassed way over the distant forest. 'There – it's up now . . . and down'. In vain he tries to pinpoint the exact place for us – not at all easy along a stretch of uniform woodland. 'Er . . . behind the big tree.' 'Which big tree?' 'By the third clump . . . in the gap . . .' 'The gap *in* the clump or *by* the clump?' 'By the . . . there it is! it's up . . .' 'In the gap?' 'No, by the tree.' 'Which tree?' '*That* tree . . . not *that* tree . . . the other tree!' 'There's thousands of trees . . .' For a split second I see it too – it's up, it's down . . . Whatever it is the wretched crows keep driving it back into cover as efficiently as if they've been paid by David Tomlinson. Tim sets up his telescope and vows he can't see anything but crows. John is waiting for Tim's decision, and Cliff and I are trying to will them to see what we'd seen. Cyril is watching the sea: 'Gannet!' Everyone tumbles head over heels and waits for instructions. 'Moving left, coming up to the big blue buoy . . . now.' It's so much easier out at sea. We could have done with a big blue buoy over the woods! Anyway, 10.12 Gannet; and at 10.18 Cyril does it again: 'Grey Plover flying right.' Got it. We try swopping over; but that was it for Benacre – both woods and sea have gone blank. Everyone back to the Saab.

'Dipper' has been sent off to Dunwich Cliffs to try to locate the scoter flock, 'Sun Grebe' is, as far as we know, at Minsmere, whilst 'Grouse' is still sitting wait-ing for Crossbills.

'Corn Bunting' is heading for Lowestoft taking in our namesake on the way. 10.39, we stop by a bit of hedge-row that looks like any other bit of hedgerow round here. We open the car doors. At last the words come true: 'Corn Bunting calling' – well, singing actually. As if to rub in how ridiculous it was to miss it last year –

another one starts singing a short way away, and, compounding the spirit of rampant optimism, a Tree Sparrow chirps from the nearest tree. At this moment we really do believe we're doing pretty well. At Benacre we'd received news from the RAF man that Radio Orwell (East Anglian local radio) had just broadcast the *Country Life* score as 109. Since they traditionally hit a hundred by 07.00, this implied that they were having problems. *Only* 109 . . . 'I don't believe it' I muttered, wishing that I did. 'How many did they say we've got?' John asked, knowing perfectly well they had no way of knowing, since we didn't know ourselves. '110' came the reply. Oh . . . we could appreciate the problem. We were supposed to 'phone in the score now and then, and we hadn't. They had to broadcast something to the thousands of anxious listeners who'd no doubt been glued to their radios since midnight. *Country Life* may well have 150 for all we know. But for the moment, ridiculous though it seems, spurious news of 109 actually encouraged us almost as much as the Corn Bunting.

The fates, however, are cruel, and so is Lowestoft traffic on a Saturday morning. It is 11.00 before we get our next bird, in a most unlikely habitat. There, grazing peacefully in the middle of the Bird's Eye car park – a Brent Goose! Does it know it's *Bird's* Eye's car park? There is of course a rule against counting captive or injured birds. This goose is clearly neither. Our Lowestoft contact, Big Brian, had reported its arrival – which is why we hadn't actually fainted when we saw it. It must have *flown* in, so it obviously isn't injured, and neither is it captive, as surely not even Bird's Eye's publicity department would keep a pet goose in a car park. Actually it is a very grassy car park, and covered in puddles and the bird looks remarkably content there. We hope *Country Life* don't know about it, but bet they do. We entertain unsporting thoughts about chasing it away – but don't. We just wish some cars would come and park – or better still half a dozen motor bikes.

11.00, *we* park as near the Goose as we dare without feeling guilty (it carries on feeding) and are greeted by Big Brian himself at our 'traditional' Black Redstart spot. This is as unlovely as most Black Redstart spots – a bunch of gas tanks and a rusty old hut. Brian informs us that the birds have been flitting to and from the hut all morning. It should be quick and easy. Half an hour

Cock Black
Redstart

Time 11.00

120 species

later we still haven't seen them. We have added Eider, another Lowestoft speciality, and Sanderling flying off shore, but the Black Redstart is becoming another Hawfinch, as it were. This is the same spot that two years ago *Country Life* failed to get Black Redstart half an hour after we'd seen it and ten minutes before the BBC filmed it! Ever since then they've gone down to Landguard for *their* Black Redstart. This is also the place that the fog rolled in the previous two years. At least that's not going to happen today; its far too breezy. There are squally showers and, at the moment, bright sunshine – surely bright enough to inspire a Black Redstart to sing. Not a squeak.

11.30, there's a cloudburst and we use it as an excuse to make a short excursion to 'knock off' Egyptian Goose. 11.36, we're at a curious little Holiday Camp with a large ornamental pool with a couple of what always look to me like ornamental birds. Apparently,

however, these Egyptian Geese are free-flying and as wild as they ever are. Both Kingfisher and Grey Wagtail have been seen here. These are both birds that have given us a lot of trouble on previous races. Two years ago we were lucky when a Kingfisher almost flew through the car, but we only had a quarter of the wagtail (John saw it – we didn't). Last year we missed both. So we give the Holiday Camp a couple of minutes. True to form we see nothing. By 11.45 we're back at Lowestoft never even imagining that Brian won't have found our Black Redstart by now. We can see him standing on the sea-wall looking as if he's about to jump off. His doleful gestures tell us the bird *still* hasn't reappeared. 'But I was watching it all morning . . . before *you* arrived!' We console Brian, rather forgetting that it's us who are going to lose! Black Redstarts have been known in other parts of Lowestoft – most of them bizarre. We drive slowly past the Woolworth's build-

A single Brent Goose 'looks remarkably content' on Bird's Eye's car park in Lowestoft.

125

ing, and peer at the roof of Marks & Spencers. We follow Brian down Commercial Road to the final possible venue – a bunch of ramshackle old warehouses. When we arrive we discover . . . they've been demolished! So that's it for Black Redstart – it's a bird we simply are not going to get.

Half an hour later we've more or less crossed off another supposed certainty: Wood Warbler. There should have been one singing at Fen Cottage, but there wasn't. Now we're in a wood to the south of Benacre where Cliff has had Wood Warbler singing during the past week. Just to make sure we dip out the sun dives behind a huge black cloud and no birds sing. Most years one can be pretty sure of Wood Warbler up at Kelling in North Norfolk – but not this year: 'not arrived yet' is the news. It's now well after mid-day and we have clearly hit one of those bad patches that any big-twitch team is surely going to experience sometime during the day. Except that such is our awe of *Country Life*'s efficiency that we believe they are immune. We can simply never imagine them missing anything that is theoretically there. Their Black Redstarts are permanently visible; their Wood Warblers wouldn't *dare* not sing. Therefore if we've failed on those birds we *must* be at least two behind. Are we paranoid? or just realistic?

12.48 and we are at last driving down the leafy lane

to Minsmere. It seems almost sacrilege to be arriving at Britain's most prolific bird reserve so late in the day. On the other hand, maybe our morale will get a much needed boost. Mind you, the fact that we *are* so late has been dictated by the news that the water is high and there probably won't be as much here as usual. On the other hand, it is now high tide and I'm hoping that what few waders there are in this part of Suffolk will have been driven off the beaches and estuaries and onto the 'scrape'. The RSPB car park is overflowing with charabancs and no doubt we'll have to queue to get into the hides; but the public rarely drive birds away from the reserve so there should be no reason to regret not timing our visit for the quieter early hours.

Anyway – enough of these theories. The fact is, we need birds, and quickly, so 'what's about?' There's plenty of information waiting for us in the reception area from our official back-up team, and friends, and from people we've never seen before. The trouble is, without wishing to sound even more paranoid, we're never quite sure whom to believe, especially as people keep contradicting one another. We are officially told 'There are two Goldeneyes on Island Mere' and 'Long-tailed Duck on the Scrape.' 'Dipper's walky-talky is broadcasting efficiently from Dunwich Cliffs: 'I'm watching a large flock of Common Scoter well out on the sea'. 'Any Velvets with them?' 'Could be . . . It's too

The female Long-tailed Duck on the Scrape at Minsmere was also seen by the *Country Life* team; it had been there for several months, but disappeared shortly after the Big Bird Race. Avocets and a family of Canada Geese are on the right.

rough to see properly and I need a better telescope.'
We *have* a better telescope but not enough time to scoot
over to Dunwich Cliffs. When we spot a single Common
Scoter immediately we reach the Minsmere shore we
decide to think ourselves lucky and leave the 'could be'
Velvets.

In the public hide there's more official back-up
waiting. The precision is positively military, aided by
Minsmere's system of marking the islands with little
numbers. It makes the place look like a shooting range.
'Long-tailed Duck in front of 44' . . . got it! 'Wigeon on
47' . . . aim telescopes and . . . got that too. 'Right,
13.00, better get moving!' 'Is that *it*?' I think . . . Last
year we really *enjoyed* Minsmere, and actually *found*
several birds nobody else even saw: Med. and Glaucous
Gulls, a Hen Harrier flying over, and Pied Flycatcher –
it was proper birdwatching! Tim and I try to rebel
mildly and continue to scan the scrape, but we have to
admit there *is* nothing else there, least of all any
waders. They'd been right – the water *is* high.

We scramble out of the public hide and have to run
along the sand to catch up with John and Cliff. It's
hot now, the sun is blazing and yet I'm still wearing the
extra sweater I'd put on for the night shift . . . and now
we're having to run! For once in my life, I'm not
enjoying Minsmere. It really is a shame to have to do
it quickly; in fact it's impossible. It's quite a trek between hides unless you have motorbikes. I now recall
a rumour that there *were* motorbikes tazzing around
here last night – *Country Life*? . . . surely not?

Anyway . . . where are we going next? asks one of our
back-up boys, anxious that we don't go off wandering
as is our wont. 'Island Mere, for Goldeneye'. 'Don't
bother, there aren't any!' 'But we've just been told
there are!' 'Well, there aren't; I've just been there . . .
they weren't Goldeneye. What *were* they then? . . .
'Any Ruddy Duck?' 'No.' 'Has the Jack Snipe been
seen lately? It's been in front of the hide some days?'
'No.' I almost get the feeling someone doesn't want us
to go to the Island Mere. We make further enquiries of
anyone who cares to answer: 'Any sign of the Med.
Gull?' 'No.' 'Any waders . . . godwits?' 'There were
both godwits earlier in the day . . . but they've gone
now. *They* saw them . . .' I don't *think* we are being
taunted, but of course *They* are *Country Life*. We are

also told that *They* were on 128 at 12.00. We are on about 125 at 13.00. Clearly we are, as usual, way behind, and Minsmere isn't going to help much. At this moment I think we feel, well, . . . confused. My instincts tell me to go to the Island Mere and have a go for ourselves, but the clock and several people tell us not to. Perhaps we should go and try for the Crossbills which we've just been told John Burton has in fact found again? Or perhaps not. John suddenly appears himself and is telling us that in fact 'Grouse' has had nothing but a Long-tailed Tit all morning! What *is* going on? Maybe someone didn't want us at Minsmere at all. (I am of course a fully registered member of Paranoids Anonymous.)

13.30 We are back at Angel Cottage just long enough to hear more confusing news from north Norfolk. 'There are three good birds at Snettisham.' 'What are they?' 'Don't know.' We get back into the Land Rover and go for a quick spin round another of Cliff's flood-pools by the Blyth in search of some of these damned elusive waders. The 'spin' is about as smooth as the big dipper at Blackpool. Come to think of it, the big dipper is what our team is becoming! At least our luck is consistent now – lousy. Last night there were both godwits and a Whimbrel here. The tide is high and the birds ought to have been forced off the mud onto the pools; but they haven't. Presumably they are tucked up somewhere fast asleep in a secret roosting place even Cliff doesn't know about. Or maybe they're hiding behind a bank and laughing at us. 13.46, a single Curlew lets itself be seen – I bet he gets in trouble with his mates. It's 14.00 now – we've been at it twelve hours – half a day! – and we realise we still haven't seen a Cormorant. This is a species that with any luck at all we would have just seen flying over sometime as we toured the coast. As Cliff remarks: 'Things must be bad if we have to search for Cormorant!' 14.02, Cormorant sitting on a post about a mile away – thought we couldn't see you, didn't you?

The Big Dipper careers back to Angel Cottage and I can't help admitting I'll enjoy the rather classier comfort of the Saab Turbo for the rest of the day. Earlier on we'd figured that it'd be nice to be leaving here at about 13.00 with about 140. In fact it's now just after 14.00 and we've got less than 130. We must be

Time 13.00

Time 14.00

The lovely estuary near Blythburgh: Shelducks dabble while two Cormorants dry themselves in the sun.

miles behind. Lying by the cottage 'phone are notes from Norfolk 'Titchwell – Little Gulls and Baird's Sandpiper! . . .' Britain's first spring record? 'Cley – Spoonbill, Kentish Plover, Little Ringed Plover and maybe Temminck's Stint.' There's no mention of commoner waders. We hope this is because they assume we don't need them, *not* because they're not there! In fact we still need both godwits, Whimbrel, Ruff, Knot, Little Stint, Curlew Sandpiper, Wood and Green Sandpiper – all of which we've had on previous years. Surely *some* of them must be in north Norfolk!? I am feeling a bit dozy – it tends to happen when things aren't going so well – and I ask John if he'd care to take over the driving for the Norfolk run. It's only now that I've driven for half the day (less really, since we kept swapping vehicles) that I realise just what a fantastic job John did driving for the whole of the previous year's races. He tends to drive faster than me – legal, but fast – and he's actually rather looking forward to handling the Turbo, so it's a good move. There's

almost a sense of release and freedom as we cruise away
from Suffolk on the road to Norwich. Mind you, our
mood is tainted by the knowledge that we are about to
attempt two of our traditional 'bogey' species on the
way north: Kingfisher and Grey Wagtail. Surely we're
due for a change of luck? Apparently not. About 14.15
we call in at a Kingfisher site where we're expecting
to be met by one of our 'informers' – no informer, no
Kingfisher. Ten minutes later we stop at a barn where
Barn Owl pellets have been found recently. Plenty of
pellets . . . no owl. Will we see *any* more birds today?
Everything seems to be getting on our nerves – and our
tail. There's now a police car behind us making sure
we don't attempt David Tomlinson's 69.44 m.p.h.
average speed. Not that we'd do anything naughty of
course, but it's hard to ignore the obvious power of the
Turbo. As we pass through a village and drop to thirty
it feels like we're going backwards. At 14.40 we're
slowing down again as we approach a gravel pit. What's
this? Grey Wagtail? No, Little Ringed Plover. Cliff

reckons it's not safe to rely on seeing the birds supposedly at Cley. We all agree. Cliff points out the likely
places. 'They were displaying down there on the "spit",
then they flew into that field.' John and I go down to
the gravel while Tim and Cliff scan the field. Meanwhile we all note Great Crested Grebe – at 14.44 . . . at
least that's *one* more. Suddenly John yells – 'L.R.P.!'
The bird flies from the spit to the field calling all the
way, just like it rehearsed. 14.48. Four minutes – that's
what it ought to be like. In our paranoid visions all
Country Life site-stops are as quick as this. In truth –
they probably *are*!

Time 15.00

15.01 and we're going round the Norwich by-pass
quickly and smoothly. Norwich City are playing
Brighton, but the fans are safely locked up inside and
since they've been playing nearly a minute they're
probably beating each other up by now to relieve the
boredom. We should be away from town before they're
thrown out and block up the road again.

Now that we're riding smoothly in the Saab, Tim
has at last been able to fill in his score sheet. We're on
129 at just after 15.00. 'They' were on 128 three hours
ago. As if that's not depressing enough, we're about to
go for Grey Wagtail – a bird we *never* get. Well it's worse
than that, actually. Two years ago John saw it dis-
appearing upstream and the rest of us waited half an
hour failing to relocate it. Last year we failed to see it
again, at the same place.

Great Crested
Grebe

There are in fact lots of water mills in East Anglia all
looking as if they were built as ideal homes for Grey
Wagtails. Strangely 99.9% of them are wagtail-less.
Why the one we're going to now should be anything
else I don't know. John Burton in the 'Grouse' back-up
vehicle had been tailing us for some way on our drive
north. We couldn't really see the point of this. We
wanted people to go ahead, not to follow us. So we'd
sent him ahead to 'Something-ton' Mill to check out
the wagtails. Either Grouse could 'sit on it' or save us
time by telling us that, as usual, it isn't there. 15.22,
'Corn Bunting' sees 'Grouse' . . . thumbs up . . . 'Corn
Bunting' sees Grey Wagtail! As if to make up for
previous years, there are two, immediately visible,
prancing about just below the bridge.

130 species

As we zoom off, we contemplate the fact that *this* is
the way to use a back-up vehicle. Send them ahead;

make sure to agree a rendezvous point; and show us the bird or say it's not there. It seems simple enough. On the other hand, we'd've seen the wagtails instantly for ourselves. Never mind . . . it feels like team-work and it's rather nice. Of course *Country Life* do it all the time. It's now 15.30 and the second Saab is literally leading us to north Norfolk. John remarks that it's also nice to be led by another car and not have to worry about directions and map reading. It gives us time to have a little think. The Little Ringed Plover and the Grey Wagtail have cheered us up. We feel we must be well behind; but then we were last year. *Country Life* are traditionally fast starters and we're traditionally good finishers . . . well, we were last year! Anyway it usually turns out that they're not as far ahead as we assume they are. We feel strangely philosophical . . . we might even just enjoy the last hours or so of daylight, whilst always hoping for a 'late-run'.

A Combined Harvester blocking the road ahead jolts us from our reverie. We squeeze past, anxious not to lose the Saab that's supposedly leading us – but to where? It's decision time. Are we going to Snettisham and Hunstanton and working east to Cley – or vice versa? We discuss the pros and cons. Snettisham is an RSPB Reserve where the warden is notoriously 'close' to the *Country Life* team. Two years ago we went there and were victims of withheld information. A bunch of Snettisham regulars assured us there was 'nothing about' while hoping we wouldn't see the Spoonbill sleeping out on the mudflats behind us. We didn't. We know there are three good birds at Snettisham, but we don't know what they are, and we fear that if we go there no-one's going to tell us! Paranoid? We may be . . . How about Hunstanton? Nothing to see there now except Fulmar. 'Can't we get that at Weybourne?' (near Cley). Someone says 'yes'. Cley is often a good place to be at the end of the day to 'mop up' bits and pieces. Then again, the news isn't very exciting from there. Cley *is* however an excellent centre of information for the whole coast. If we get there quickly we can get a full briefing and there should be time to dash about quite a bit before dark. We decide to go straight to Cley. 'Corn Bunting' informs 'Grouse' of the decision and the leading Saab whips us along a devious but efficient route towards Cley.

Time 16.00

Just after 16.00 we are on the outskirts of Holt. We veer off towards Weybourne to tick off Fulmar. As we approach the village, Tim, whom I suspect must have been asleep for a while, asks 'Why are we going here?' 'Fulmar.' 'There's no Fulmars here. The cliffs are too low.' I'm convinced somebody said 'yes' a while back. Perhaps Tim was being seduced in his dreams. John is either on my side or trying to cheer me up. 'I reckon we'll be able to look up the coast towards Sheringham' – where there definitely *are* Fulmars. 'Anyway' says Cliff 'we're here now; we might as well have a look' (this could be the *ffPS* catch-phrase!). We park and look up the coast through the heat-haze. There are gulls shimmering on the beach way in the distance, and white birds going in and out of the cliffs. More gulls practising their gliding? Tim sets up his telescope and is clearly relieved that he may be proved wrong . . . 'Yep . . . I think they're Fulmars.' 'Well, this one definitely is!' I add almost smugly as a single bird swoops right over our heads. So . . . there *are* Fulmars at Weybourne. Well, one; and that's enough.

That was 16.07. At 16.15 we arrive at Cley with a score of 130. If we're really lucky it could shoot up by ten in the next half hour. What we need now is information, but where's our back-up team? The fact is, none of us quite remembers what the exact arrangement was, but surely everyone was supposed to meet up at Cley! Or did we say Titchwell? . . . or Hunstanton? Most of

131 species

A Fulmar planes along the shore at Weybourne.

them left long before we'd decided which way to do the Norfolk Coast. As we look frantically for help at 16.15 I think we blamed everyone except ourselves. Looking back now, it was surely our fault. At Whalsey Hill we pass the *Country Life* back-up squad. Half a dozen cars, various aerials and several awfully confident faces. They wave as we go past. We turn into the Norfolk Naturalist Trust's car park by the official reception to the Cley Reserve. Lots of cars, but we don't recognise any of them. Oh yes we do . . . a small black and white mini disguised as a Panda, the symbol of the World Wildlife Fund. Mark Carwardine – and here he comes now. Mark is feeling as bemused as we are. 'Where's everybody else? I thought other people were meeting me . . . I've been on my own all day.' We sympathise for several seconds. 'So did we. What's about?' 'Spoonbill, Pintail. What do you need?' 'Waders . . .' 'Which ones?' 'Most of them; godwits . . . oh, and Lesser Whitethroat!' Amazingly Mark had an instant reply: 'In the bushes by the road.' I'm already in the public hide by the car park: 16.25, Spoonbill and Pintail. Everyone sees them. Into the car again. Down to the East Bank. 'Is this really the best place for waders?' I ask. Mark assures us it is and Tim confirms it. The rest of the reserve is either very wet or there's been a lot of digging going on. Consequently what few waders there are have been frequenting the pool at the sea end of the East Bank, just like they used to back in the fifties before

ffPS

BILL ODDIE

See picture on
p. 82

132 species
133 species

134 species

Cley reserve acquired its carefully managed scrapes and lagoons and its half dozen or so hides. Earlier in the day there'd been both godwits and a Kentish Plover exactly where we are now looking. The story is the same as at Benacre and Minsmere – 'You should have been here earlier.'

16.33. Four consolation Whimbrel fly over. I'm all for giving Cley a chance and not hurrying away as we had done at Minsmere. We look over to the North Hide – twenty minutes walk there and back at least. Shall we? Even as we step northward our way is barred by an unknown 'helper': 'Nothing at the North Hide . . . I've just come back from there.' As at Minsmere – we believe him (do we ever learn?) and set off back to the East Bank. Passing birders give us more news. More positive this time. Actually I think I trust the folks at Cley more than I do at Minsmere. 'Snettisham: Great Grey Shrike, Melodious Warbler' and something less amazing. (I can't remember what, but whatever it was we'd already got it.) 'Holkham: Pied Flycatcher and Hoopoe' which the resourceful Mark Carwardine had in fact found for us. So maybe *Country Life* don't know about them. Talking of *Them*, we also hear a rumour that half an hour ago they were on 136. We're now on 134. Can it be so close? I don't believe it.

Even as we reach the road the neurotic scream of a nearly airborne Porsche shatters the peace of the Marshes. Tomlinson and crew flash past us so fast it's almost subliminal. They leave the sound of their confidence echoing on the breeze, as they wave us 'goodbye' and 'good luck'. They don't look like a team who are only on 136! Ageing 'dudes' hurl themselves into the safety of the roadside gorse bushes as the Porsche threatens to flatten them like the coyote in the Road Runner cartoons . . . 'Beep beep . . . brum brum . . . swooosh.' If they'd only known we were still looking for Lesser Whitethroat they would have laughed so much they'd have probably skidded off into the North Sea and floated away to Holland. Perhaps that's where they're going. Maybe the Porsche converts into a hovercraft like one of James Bond's cars. Actually James Bond drives a Saab Turbo – like us – so there!

Nevertheless, we still can't find a Lesser Whitethroat in the bushes. Yes, we know . . . 'We should have been here earlier.'

Dude: see p. 64

16.59 and we're almost hurrying to Dawkes hide, still at Cley. To our left are a bunch of grazing Grey-lags and amongst them . . . a White-fronted Goose? Oh . . . four White-fronts. They look wild enough . . . so down they go. Actually one of them's a bit small isn't it? Tim recounts the tale. Apparently this bird was first seen in February and identified as a Lesser White-front. It was then examined and reassessed and finally pronounced a 'probable hybrid'. It is exactly the sort of bird I find fascinating and would love to have a good long look at. Alas, all that matters for the moment is: we can't count it. Into the hide. Here are two visible godwits. One to the left. One to the right. The one on the left is a Bar-tailed; the one on the right is a Black-tailed. O.K., so we'll get them in singles! Here are other birders in the hide amiably forthcoming with information. 'Any Ruff?' 'No.' 'Kentish Plover? Knot?' . . . 'Not for a while', and 'Not at all' 'Oh . . . three Cranes flew over this morning'. I honestly don't think he even knew we were on the 'Big Bird Race'. He was just a birder sharing his excitement. I envied him.

17.15, we're travelling west to Holkham to have a go for Mark's Pied Fly and Hoopoe. 17.30-ish, we arrive. Holkham Pines is not a place you can do in a couple of minutes. They are about 100 yards wide and two miles long, and looking for a single bird in them is 'needle in a haystack' time. We assume there's someone there to meet us. There isn't. Then I remember . . . we're supposed to use the new technology . . . 'Corn Bunting calling . . . anyone here?' I get an immediate reply: 'Sun Grebe to Corn crackle . . . pop . . . squeak . . . thud'. Nothing. Has 'Sun Grebe' been attacked by a giant Pied Flycatcher? Come to think of it – who *is* Sun Grebe? Whoever he is, he's no bloody help now. We wander off grumpily into Holkham Woods. If we can't even find our back-up team, what chance do we have with a Pied Fly!

A few minutes later Mark Carwardine, whose panda mini understandably lags some way behind our black panther Saab, catches up with us. 'The Hoopoe was along here this morning, and so was the Pied Fly.' Fine . . . but where are they *now*? At least we've instinctively chosen the right area. We could so easily have gone in the other direction and been half way to Wells by now, and no-one would ever have found us. Now

135 species
Time 17.00

136 species
137 species

Bar-tailed Godwit (*above*) and Black-tailed Godwit

someone else finds us . . . another friend: 'Pied Fly . . . it's still here.' We hurry up the path to where four or five of our back-up cast are squatting on the dunes staring at the trees. We refrain from suggesting that it might have been more efficient if one of them had waited for us at the car park. The group includes the two blondes we last saw back at Ginger Bread Cottage. They are no longer wearing parrots on their hats. We feel it would be churlish to grumble. They've no doubt suffered quite enough already. Big Bird Race?! . . . they'd hardly moved all bleedin' day! Seen *one* bird – a ruddy Pied Fly! Yes, but that's the one we need. It is no longer visible, but as we stare through holes in the foliage our last 'silly bird' gives itself up – a Lesser Whitethroat sings at 17.49. Suddenly I see a flitting movement at the back of the leaf canopy. 'That's it!' Tim tempers optimism with conscience. 'Maybe.' 'Well, it's a Flycatcher.' It was indeed. Tim scrambles down the bank and through the other side of the trees. It goes quiet. We follow him and meet up. 'Did you see it?' 'Yes. It's a Spotted . . .' I don't feel too embarrassed. To get the family right on that view was fairly efficient. A minute later Tim finds the Pied. John sees it. So do I. Cliff takes a nerve wracking minute longer. 'Third branch left . . . under the brown leaves . . . dropped down . . . flitted up again.' 'Got it.' 17.51, Pied Flycatcher.

138 species

139 species

We work back to the car via the Hoopoe spot. Hoopoes are funny birds. Some of them sit on vicars' lawns for weeks on end; others appear and disappear like conjurors' rabbits. It was certainly no reflection on Mark that we couldn't re-locate this one. He'd done very well to find it in the first place. We didn't find the strangulated 'Sun Grebe' either. I *think* it was Tim Parmenter, in which case I saw him safe and well a few hours later so that's O.K.

Three minutes to six. We are now on 139 and heading for Overy Staithe or is it Burnham Overy? There seems to be some small confusion. Mark has passed on news to us of Whooper Swan (a funny date, come to think of it, but it didn't strike us at the time), Whinchat and Knot. Three new birds in one go . . . that's the sort of thing we need, but *quickly* please. Is there anyone there to meet us? Yes. Now all we have to do is decide where 'there' is. The description is: 'Turn right by the mill, and go along the raised bank.' The problem is there are at least two windmills along here, and three or four raised banks. We choose a mill, and a bank, and climb over a stile to go along it. As we do so we have one of the few pieces of real good luck we have enjoyed so far. At 18.07 a Kingfisher flashes past us *and* we all see it. As if to make sure we do, it lands on a post, dives into the Mill Pond and comes up with a fish. We applaud, and

Time 18.00

140 species

A Kingfisher rests at Overy Staithe.

literally run down the raised bank in a fit of misplaced optimism.

Quarter of an hour later we radio back to 'Grouse', who have been dutifully accompanying us since Cley. We can see no swans, Whinchats, Knots or people meeting us. 'Grouse' tell us why: 'Wrong Mill.' We run back to the car, which is not easy at this time of day or at this time of life. Personally I'm not feeling at all well, though Cliff literally vaults the stile and inspires us all. He's right – three birds here . . . that'll make 143 . . . Titchwell to come, where we'll get Little Gull and with any luck one or two new waders . . . we may be able to nip in at Snettisham, and we know there's Dotterel on the way . . . so that could be two or three more. Since it's nice and sunny it should be a late dusk . . . we'll try and be at Wicken for the Spotted Crake and maybe the Hobby . . . *and* we should still be able to get back with an hour to spare to have another go at Nightjar and Barn Owl . . . So let's see, if we have a really good finish, that would bring us up to 150. We'd been predicting a low score so surely 150 would win it? Would it?

Well . . . read on.

As we skid onto the muddy car park by Overy Staithe quay at about 18.10 our mood is definitely optimistic. We really do feel we have a chance of winning. An hour later we're certain we've lost. First there's a moment's trepidation that we might still be at the wrong place. Where's the mill? Here *is* a raised bank, but why didn't they say 'by the quay'?, and where are the people meeting us? Our travelling back-up lean on their cars dangerously near to a pub that must be even more dangerously near to opening time. We scamper off down the bank. A quarter of a mile we go, scanning for birds and birdwatchers. Nothing. Suddenly a young couple appear at our side . . . birders. We don't know them but they have the information. 'There was a Knot out there on the estuary . . . the Whinchat was further along the bank on the left . . . and there was a pair of Whooper Swans out on the Marsh on the right.' . . . I don't like all this past tense . . . 'Was . . . was . . . was' . . . How long ago? . . . last year? Even 'this morning' doesn't encourage us much. What we need is *now*.

We walk on to the bend indicated by the couple. No Whinchat. No swans. There are a few waders skittering ahead of us out on the estuary being driven away by the rising tide. Even as we raise telescopes, a motor boat zooms straight at the birds. Is that David Tomlinson at the helm? The waders are airborne now and heading for the sea. Frantically and hopefully we identify them . . . 'Dunlin . . . Dunlin . . . there's a bigger one . . .'. 'Grey Plover.' 'No, the other one' . . . 'Turnstone'. No matter how inadequate the view becomes we can't turn any of them into Knot. The tideline is racing higher and more motor boats appear just to make sure no waders try to sneak back and surrender themselves.

We ask the couple again. *Where* was the Whinchat? 'Further on'. We go further on. It's not there. 'And where were the swans?' 'Round the next bend.' Round the bend is exactly where we're going. We've now come nearly a mile. Two white heads pop up from a ditch on the right out on the Marsh. We don't even raise our binoculars. Their arched necks tell us: Mute Swans. Coincidence or 'string'? 'Where exactly did you see the Whoopers?' We turn to ask the young couple who, String: see p. 70 having led us a mile and a half, have now . . . vanished! After a final look round the final bend we turn grumpily and attempt to run back to the quay. My binocular strap has now worn a scarlet groove in the back of my neck, my telescope keeps whacking me in the ribs, and my wellies are welded to my feet with congealed sweat. We are disgruntled that our back-up team has let us waste so much time looking for birds that aren't here. Maybe they never were? Our paranoia is working overtime. We ask Mark 'Who saw the Whooper Swans? Did *you*?' 'No. A young couple told me. A blonde guy and a girl.' Right. Did Mark *know* them? 'I know the girl, she's a pretty good birder. I didn't know the bloke.' Was there any significance in the fact that the bloke had done *all* the talking? 'Just a little further . . . round the next bend . . . keep going . . . whoosh!' Vanished. Actually I suspect it was just the usual story. 'We should have been there earlier . . .' It was now late. Almost 19.00. We'd 'waited' nearly an hour, completely disrupted our potential schedule and severely cut down our options. **Time** 19.00

19.10. A major consolation. If, at the end of a hard day, you have to sit and ponder your mistakes there is no nicer place to do it than the RSPB reserve at Titchwell. Especially on a lovely sunny evening. At the

141 species

See picture on
p. 80

142 species

143 species

reception area there is a complete reunion of all our back-up forces. 'Grouse', 'Sun Grebe', whom we feared lost at Holkham, and even good old 'Dipper'. Perhaps we *did* say we'd meet them here and not Cley. Seeing them again reminds us what a lovely bunch they are and how hard they've worked. All grumps and grumbles are forgotten.

There is no fantastic news at Titchwell. The Baird's Sandpiper flew long ago (if indeed it was ever here; Sanderling 'string' is suspected). In any event *Country Life* didn't see it either. There are, as predicted, Little Gulls, and at 19.14 we're enjoying watching them – at least half a dozen juveniles and a superb adult. 'Grouse' has already scurried on down to the beach and is radioing back. 'There's waders here; what do you need?' 'Knot, Ruff, Little Stint . . .' 'We've got Grey Plover, Turnstone, Sanderling.' 'Sorry we've had them.' That's what we'd needed at Overy Staithe – someone telling us 'Don't bother.' We sit overlooking the reserve hoping that something will fly over. At 19.26 it does. John suddenly yells 'Osprey!' You don't have to be on a 'Bird Race' to find this a thrilling moment. A dot in the east becomes larger. Every tern and gull on the marsh scatters as the Osprey circles above them. Suddenly below it another big bird gleaming in the evening sun . . . what on earth's that? A free-flying Bar-headed Goose! (What a pity it doesn't count). Osprey and Bar-headed Goose in the air in the same view – never seen *that* before! John has – at Bharatpur in India! Cliff admits he *still* hasn't seen it, and for a horrifying moment I realise he hasn't 'latched on' to the Osprey yet. I snatch his binoculars from his eyes, and point almost vertically above his head. 'There!' 'Oh . . . I didn't realise it was so close!' Maybe the fact that we're now resigned to being 'beaten opponents' again allows us to enjoy this bit of real birdwatching. It was the best moment of the day.

Followed by one of the worst. We have now learnt to leave our walky-talkies switched on. A crackly voice asks: 'Do you still need Whinchat?' You bet we do. 'Well there's one just dropped down 50 yards from us.' 'Where are you?' '100 yards from *you*!' So they are. It's John and Mark a little further down the bank and looking our way. It therefore follows that the Whinchat is 50 yards from us too. Apparently it was, but it's dropped amongst the bushes on the marsh across a wide ditch, so we can't 'go and get it'. We'll have to wait for it to pop up again and perch. For fifteen minutes we stare. We walk up and down the bank. We climb on one another's shoulders and glare through our telescopes . . . but, like no other Whinchat known to science, it never again popped up and perched on anything. Presumably it had in fact slipped away over the bank without us seeing it go, but for the moment we suspected it had been bribed!

20.00. More time 'wasted', and it is getting distinctly dusky. There's not enough light left for any major trips now – no Snettisham, and we won't make Wicken before it's dark. We stroll back, still hoping for a bit of extra luck. Two Golden Plover fly over just before we arrive. Maybe they've landed in those distant fields with the Lapwings. No. We had Whinchats on those fences last year. Not this. Perhaps a Green or Wood Sandpiper will flit over – they always call if they do. Not today. There are no other 'extras' . . . no Black Terns, no stints. Our back-up team have been endearingly efficient here though, and they crown their performance by sending a runner to fetch six cans of beer. We drink it leaning on the Saab, and contemplating the final hours or so, at least two of which will be needed to drive back to the finishing line, in the dark. An isolated purple cloud hangs in the distance in an otherwise blue sky. Beside it, a rainbow climbs out of the horizon above Titchwell marshes. If the Osprey had had any sense of aesthetics it would have flown back for a second look.

20.05. As we leave Titchwell we hear that not long ago *Country Life* were on 143 – but how long ago? Or is it Radio Orwell having to invent the score again?! We're on 143 now – is it really this close? I still don't believe it. At least we're more or less certain of 144.

20.16, and we join a little gathering of cars and birders overlooking a very large grassy field. It doesn't look like a typical Dotterel habitat, whilst a large dry stubbly area nearby *does*. Nevertheless, they're in here somewhere. Indeed, we can see several tiny little eyebrowed heads peeping over the greenery about 150 yards away. Tim climbs on top of a van and sets up his telescope just to make sure somebody's not just trying to cheer us up by passing off Red-legged Partridge. Or

Time 20.00

Osprey (*above*) and Bar-headed Goose

maybe they're all Sociable Plover! No . . . 'they *are* Dotterel.' Apparently there's ten of them in there. They keep bobbing up and down but we certainly see at least half a dozen up at the same time. One of our birding guides who's been 'sitting on them' says: 'Bit late aren't you? I was just about to give you up.' Glad he didn't.

Actually we always seem to evoke sympathy in North Norfolk. News of our 'Whinchat problem' has clearly spread. (It is definitely becoming this year's Corn Bunting). Another car skids to a halt. 'Down by the main farm buildings . . . first left, turn left and on the right . . . Whinchat just popped up on the fence.' Just flown in from Titchwell no doubt! We're so anxious we leap into the car without really having taken in the instructions: 'First what? . . . right? . . . left? . . . where?' We can't see any farm buildings and we're at a turning. 'Follow the tyre marks.' They lead to a farm. We stop, get out and scan in the increasing gloom. Any sensible Whinchat would be snoozing by now, but if this *is* the Titchwell bird it clearly isn't at all sensible. John announces almost to himself: 'There's a little bird on the fence in front of the milk tanker.' It's nearly two hundred yards away. Tim and I slap telescopes on it

and agree: 'It is . . . it's not a bright one but it is . . .'
As if aware that we might be fooling ourselves we creep
closer making sure that Cliff has seen the bird even if,
at this distance in this light, it's hardly identifiable.
Eventually we get back in the car and drive right up to
it. It stays on the fence and nods to us. A dowdy female
but a Whinchat nevertheless, and very welcome too.

20.30. We're on 145. Daylight birding is finished
really, earlier perhaps than usual. Last year we were
stumbling round Cley at dusk hoping to trip over a
Golden Plover – which two of us did. Still, it's not over
yet. What can we *hear* on the way back south? Before
we can discuss the matter the 'Grouse' car belts past us
and John Burton yells 'I'm being bleeped.' Sounds
painful! We remember that a 'bleep' means there's hot
news been 'phoned in to Angel Cottage. Surely it's some
comment on our day that the first and only 'hot news'
comes five minutes before it gets dark! We follow John
to a 'phone-box. A minute later he emerges with the
'hot news'. 'Dotterel in north Norfolk.' In a way it's a
relief. If it *had* been something new it would surely be
too late to go and see it, but no doubt we would have
tried, and risked getting back late. It could have been
an awful decision.

Three of the
Dotterel that were
seen by both
teams in a field of
winter corn at
Ringstead.

145 species

145

20.45. We now have to make another awful decision. We can go back to the cottage directly, and we should arrive about 22.30-ish. That will leave us an hour and a half in the field, during which we can have another go at Barn Owl and Nightjar. Our back-up team are sent back to Suffolk to listen for Nightjar, whilst we consider the other possibility, which is . . . We can go to Wicken Fen. We'll arrive too late for the possible Hobby but should get the almost certain Spotted Crake, and there are Barn Owls there too. 'Four pairs on the Reserve' says Tim, 'sometimes seen flying round the car park.' 'How long will it take to drive to Wicken?' 'About an hour.' So we should get there by ten o'clock. 'And how long back from Wicken to the finish?' 'I'd like two hours' pleads John, the driver. 'So how many minutes will we have to hear the Spotted Crake?' None. Tim explains that may be all we'll need! 'If the wind's in the right direction, you can hear it from the car park.' And if it isn't? 'We'll need to walk down the track a little – about 100 yards.' 'O.K. let's say we give it ten minutes. John . . . will we get back by midnight?' 'Probably'.

I calculate that, by David Tomlinson's new lateness rule, if we're ten minutes after 12 o'clock, we'll have to count back 100 minutes, which would be 10.20 so if we've heard the Crake at 10.10 – we won't lose it! After last year there might be some justice if we won that way! But is it so close that we really might win with 146? Cliff thinks maybe. I think definitely not. I reckon that *Country Life* will score over 150. Who's right? Read on . . .

We drive in a generally southerly direction debating the choices and constantly changing our minds. Should we vote? Tim thinks we already have, assuming that it's three to one against Wicken – he being the one. We deny that any such decision has been made and point out that the road we're on is, if anything, going more to Wicken than Blythburgh . . . on the other hand, if we *do* want to go straight back . . . A thought strikes me, and I express it: 'Are there any Nightjar sites *on the way back*?' Apparently there are . . . in fact, 'we'll be passing one in about ten minutes!' . . . Oh! and 'by the way, Golden Pheasants are often seen crossing the road we're on at this very minute!' 'Shall we stop then?' 'Er, maybe . . . no . . . yes.' If our thinking appears a little less than decisive at this point it should be remembered we have been up for nearly twenty hours and we're a little emotional at the thought of losing again.

At about 21.00 we spend ten minutes clattering around some rhododendrons failing to see Golden Pheasants. Twenty minutes later we're failing to hear Nightjars. In fact, ironically, we have to admit that for once we've arrived somewhere too early! It's such a clear evening it's still surprisingly light. In another twenty minutes or so there might well be Nightjars here . . . 'but then we'd never make Wicken in time.' Aha . . . does this mean we've made a decision? Apparently . . . yes. We *are* going to Wicken. Tim almost perversely asks 'Why?' John claims it is a democratic decision. Tim, rather more realistically, suggests it's because we've driven so far down the Wicken road while trying to make up our minds that it's now too late to go straight to Suffolk instead. Cliff, ever optimistic, claims its because its the 'boldest gamble'. Maybe we'll get the crake *and* Barn Owl, *and* still get back with five minutes to spare in which we'll get Nightjar at Walberswick. Maybe . . .

I've got a big flashlight in the car meant for owl spotting. At 21.30 we are passing temptingly near to the Ouse Washes . . . we could go and dazzle an injured Bewick's Swan! (There always seems to be one left behind each spring.) We're being 'silly' of course, but there'd be no point anyway. 'Injured birds don't count.' We are reminded of the incongruous Brent Goose at Lowestoft. *Was* it injured? 'No, no' John asserts, 'it was very fit indeed. During the hour we were looking for Black Redstart it walked from one end of the car park to the other.'

21.55, and our Saab is guided by a little signpost proclaiming 'Wicken Fen Nature Reserve.' What happens next sort of sums up our day. We park, get out, and listen for the 'swish' of a distant Spotted Crake . . . for about two seconds. Silence. Tim hurries off into the blackness presumably guiding us down the 100-yards track. On we slosh for at least half a mile, or do distances seem longer at night? We stop again and strain our ears. Is the wind in the wrong direction? No. Frankly it's blowing from the marsh straight in our faces. If there are any crakes calling they ought to deafen us. Ironically there are birds audible even now that we thought might prove difficult at the start of the day – Wigeon whistling and Snipe drumming, and suddenly . . . 'swish'! – 'There it is!' I hardly have the heart to tell John and Tim that its Cliff doing one of his impersonations! The day has come full circle. We can hear human voices approaching across the marsh. Cliff thinks he recognizes one of them. 'Sounds like Bill Urwin.' Oh come on . . . surely not *Country Life* galloping over to tell us they've just gripped us off! Tim assures us there is only one car park here and there was no Porsche in it, so it can't be them. We give the Spotted Crake twenty minutes – nothing. Are we too late again? 'No' replies Tim sadly 'It's been calling incessantly till near midnight for the past couple of weeks. It must have gone!' Gone! Gone with the Wood Warblers and the Crossbills and the Knot and the Whooper Swans and our luck. We trudge back to the car telling one another to 'keep listening for Barn Owl'. We must be joking!

22.15. Will we be back by midnight? Do we care? I calculate that since our last bird was at 20.30 we can afford to be 21 minutes late without diminishing our total! Or . . . we just might 'bump into' a Barn Owl just like we just *might* have bumped into one driving around in the early morning. Except that now we're in the Saab and I can use the amazing hand-held floodlight which plugs into the car's electric cigarette-lighter. We couldn't use it this morning, because Land Rovers don't have cigarette-lighters. I lean out of the window and flash the truly amazing beam across the passing trees and hedgerows, rousing farmers from their beds and illuminating courting couples. John spots oncoming headlights and yells 'Turn it off' so I don't blind the approaching driver. Good thing too. It's a

Time 23.00

police car! That would have been the perfect end to our day – roped in by the boys in blue for dazzling them into the ditch! Actually, flashing for Barn Owls is rather fun. It wakes us up and makes us feel – entirely falsely I'm sure – that we're still in there with a chance. Cliff remarks that he does feel better at this stage than in either of the previous years, and we agree, despite being convinced we're well behind.

23.25, and thanks to John's swift, yet legal, driving we're back in the region of Angel Cottage. Half an hour 'in the field'. Barn Owl? – no, we don't have any nearby

sites. So . . . Nightjar? We could nip back to the cottage

and find out if our back-up team has located any, but then we'd lose quarter of an hour doing so. We know one was heard 'somewhere in Dunwich Forest' last night, so we go straight there. Cliff knows the likeliest spots. We try three of them.

23.51, we give up and return home, dazzling all the way.

Midnight. It takes me several minutes to lever my congealed wellies off my truly disgusting feet. I'm hot, grubby and undeniably tired. I limp into Angel Cottage. It is packed. David Tomlinson glows from out of the motley crowd and with something resembling coyness confides that they have been back so long he's had time to wash, shave and change. In the kitchen there's Robbie, Laura, Carol Inskipp and June Waller greeting us with hugs, curry and wine and generally treating us like anything but 'defeated opponents'. The other rooms are heaving with helpers and strangers. I assume that anyone I don't recognise was on their back-up team. Partially because there's no film cameras this year, and probably also because it's a foregone conclusion, the result simply filters through to us. After eliminating the odd foreign goose and suspect duck, *Country Life* have a final score of 151. We, as we have been since 20.30, are of course 144 (excluding the Bar-headed Goose). The fact that I predicted their score pretty accurately some time back is definitely no consolation. We have been soundly drubbed.

I am genuinely curious to see their final list. I'm assuming that they've had quite a few 'rarities' – perhaps Tim will be able to get the Committee to reject some! Not at all. What I see are species we went for and missed – Wood Warbler, Black Redstart, Crossbill – plus other birds that required knowledge of specific sites – Firecrest and Woodlark. They'd obviously also had the sort of luck we'd missed out on – Green and Wood Sandpipers – one 'flying over', one 'flying away'. And Goldeneye – 'Where was that?' I ask. 'Minsmere Island Mere . . . two of them.'

My mind flashes back to 13.00. 'Don't bother with the Island Mere . . . no Goldeneye.' 'They were a bit elusive; kept coming in and out of the reeds' adds Peter Smith. My paranoia also reminds me of Overy Staithe. 'Did you go for the Whooper Swans?' I ask Bill Urwin. 'What Whooper Swans?' 'At Overy Staithe'. 'Didn't hear about those. We heard there was one flew over somewhere in the morning . . . but nothing about Overy Staithe.' If they'd really existed could it be even conceivable that *Country Life*'s super-efficient back-up wouldn't have known about them? Who *were* the mystery couple, and where are they now? . . .

'24.30'. As we nibbled our curry and didn't drink the champagne that the winning team were not obliged to share with the defeated opponents, we couldn't help pondering . . . why did we lose? Our back-up team generously tried to take the blame. I wouldn't accept that. Maybe they lacked 'experience' of the rather rigid principles that constitute maximum efficiency i.e. 'Travel ahead of the team . . . find the bird . . . somebody "sit on it" . . . someone else meet them, etc.' . . . but the fact was they'd found quite a few things for us and undoubtedly saved us some time.

My own theory is that because there were so few migrants around on the day, the event lost that element of unpredictability, luck and (dare I even suggest?) birdwatching skill that had helped us do so well last year. This year most of the birds were, in a sense, predictable – as predictable as birds can ever be. Locating them was a matter of elaborate research, and seeing a large number of them involved an almost paramilitary operation featuring accurate and widespread back-up and a taxing schedule requiring speed of car and foot. David Tomlinson himself attributed their victory to 'The Suffolk Recorders' – is that a regiment? . . . the Queen's Own Suffolk Recorders . . . an East Anglian birding equivalent to the Edinburgh Pipes?

There is another theory. The Lord may well have been punishing us for betraying our principles as 'the Gentlemen'. Back-up vehicles . . . walky-talkies . . . no cooked breakfasts! We tried to play *Country Life* at their own game and we lost, as I think we always would. But what *was* the game? Supposedly birdwatching . . . but is it? I'll think about that tomorrow . . .

Meanwhile . . . it's a.m. on Sunday morning. I was getting up twenty four hours ago. Now I'm arriving back at John Burton's cottage. I admit I'm tired . . . but am I hallucinating? I know John has a tame Barn Owl . . . that's it in its enclosure . . . but what's that on top? Come to visit its captive friend . . . a wild one! So

that's where it's been. 02.00, I am lulled to sleep by
the sound of a Barn Owl wheezing outside my window.
Or is it laughing?

Sunday. The next day. Lunchtime. The closing
ceremony. We should have held this jolly winding-
down do in the garden of a local pub. Instead the rain's
bucketing down. What if it had been like this yesterday?
That would have disrupted a few plans. Instead of
basking in the garden we're crammed sardine-like into
a wooden shed. It's like having a party in one of the
hides at Minsmere – except there's no seats. The food
is tasty, if not tasteful; being almost entirely avian! –
chicken, turkey, pheasant, pigeon. Yesterday we count
'em. Today we eat 'em!! The mood is jovial. I draw the
raffle and every bottle of Moet & Chandon seems to go
to someone from Minsmere – I guess they earned it.
John Gooders has had to rush back home to work, and
Cliff Waller has been 'unavoidably detained' – probably gone out bird-watching! Laura and I are off to
Shetland early next morning, so we want to get back
to London and pack. Farewell to Tim and Carol
Inskipp, bye-bye 'Grouse', and 'Dipper' and 'Sun
Grebe' and . . . 'au revoir' *Country Life?* –

Well . . . where *do* we go from here? Are we getting to
be bad-losers? Actually I think we're pretty good at it
– we've lost three years running. Anything I say now
will probably sound like 'sour grapes' . . . but I'm
going to say it anyway.

I have to confess I do feel some kind of puristic ethical
objection to massed back-up teams, extra vehicles,
radio-links etc, etc. However, I am aware that there
are two very sound objections to my feelings.

1. If the point of the event is sponsorship and fund-
raising (which it surely is) then the more birds that are
recorded the more money is raised. So what does it
matter what the methods are?

2. If the point of the event is to set a 24-hour birdwatching record then . . . what you see is what you see
. . . so again what does it matter what the methods are?

However, if a record *is* the point – 'how many birds
can a birdwatcher see in Britain in twenty four hours?'
– why impose rules at all? Why not use tape-recorders?
Why not start in Suffolk and end up in Shetland? Why
have four to a team? The answer in part has been

'because this is a race', an admittedly artificial publicity event to attract media interest and sponsorship.

However, though thanks to many people's great efforts and generosity we did attract considerable sponsorship for the 'Big Bird Race', the media were far less interested than in previous years. There was no coverage by television or a major newspaper. I've a feeling the event needs a new 'angle' for 1984. Perhaps a full scale 24-hour assault on the 'British Record' – anywhere, anyhow, with boats, planes, helicopters, and Saabs and Porsches waiting round every corner. Or maybe an International Race. Britain v USA has been mooted. A team of British birders has to do 24 hours in the States whilst the Americans try Suffolk, and then vice versa the following weekend. I presume we'd play by 'American rules' too, and that does appeal to me. That means no back-ups and no talking to anyone on the day except fellow team-members. I do have an instinct that it is important that whatever *Country Life* and *ffPS* get up to next spring we need to retain or perhaps even regain the approval of the 'Bird-World' in general. I know that other birders in the field on 14th May, seeing the fast cars and walky-talkies, were often rather derisive. 'Oh that's not birdwatching!' Of course, they were right. The event was more of a Commando course round check-points; more like a glorified car-rally. The check-points happened to be birds, but at times I felt we might as well have been counting sponsored lamp-posts! 'American rules' – or something even stricter – would put the birds back into the 'Bird Race' and, I think, add a little more ornithological integrity. I know all the *ffPS* team agree. Would we be talking this way if we'd won? Frankly and honestly – Yes. In fact more so . . . then nobody could accuse us of sour grapes! As it is . . . feel free . . .

Meanwhile, the 'Big Bird Race' earned over £6,000. We had a lot of fun, and I've enjoyed writing our story. *Whatever* happens next year . . . would I do it again? Certainly.

Oh, by the way, I'm still on Out Skerries. I have just seen my 75th species. It's taken me 14 days!

List of Sponsors

of present and past 'Big Bird Races'

Country Life team

Barbour
Bedfords (Swaffham)
Birds and Natural History Book Society
Collins Publishers
Country Life
Esso
Haith's Bird Foods
Hayter
Humberts
Jackson-Stopps and Staff
Leitz Instruments
Martini and Rossi
McAlpine Humberoak
Mercedes Benz (UK)
Moet et Chandon
Newton and Godin
Pace Petroleum
Phillips, the auctioneers
Pirelli
Porsche Cars (GB)
Pyser (Swift binoculars)
Richard Green (art gallery)
Roy Miles (art gallery)
Rudolph Agnew
Savills
Shell
Thorntons Special Toffees
Todd Research
Tradecoaters
Tryon and Moorland Gallery
Waterlow (Dunstable)

ffPS team

Alecto Historical Editions
André Deutsch
Bayer (UK)
Bovis International
British Petroleum
Bruce Coleman
Camera Care Systems
Collins Publishers
Dragon Entertainments
Eurobooks
Eyre Methuen
Fuller's Brewery
Goldcrest Films and Television
Gulf Oil
Ilford Films
Living Countryside
Lloyd's Bank
National Westminster Bank
Pace Petroleum
Paul's Agriculture
Philips Lamps
Reader's Digest
Royal Air Force
Saab (UK)
Sabers of Norwich
Sanyo (UK)
Scene (Sunday Times)
Suntory
Town and Gown Travel (Peregrine Holidays)
Van Den Berghs (Stork Brands)
Wildlife Magazine
Zeiss (West Germany)

List of Species

recorded by the teams
in 1980, 1981, 1982 and 1983

Black squares indicate
genuinely wild or feral
species seen and/or heard
by all four team members.

Grey squares indicate
species presumed to have
escaped from captivity.

Asterisks indicate species
seen and/or heard, but not
by the whole team.

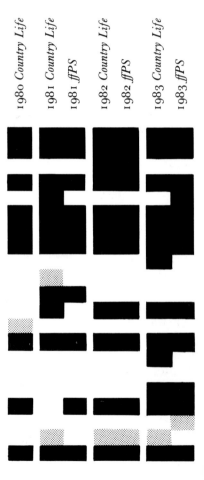

	1980 Country Life	1981 Country Life	1981 ffPS	1982 Country Life	1982 ffPS	1983 Country Life	1983 ffPS
Little Grebe							
Great Crested Grebe							
Black-necked Grebe							
Fulmar							
Gannet							
Cormorant							
Bittern							
Grey Heron							
White Stork							
Sacred Ibis							
Glossy Ibis							
Spoonbill							
Chilean Flamingo							
Mute Swan							
Bean Goose							
Pink-footed Goose							
White-fronted Goose							
Greylag Goose							
Bar-headed Goose							
Snow Goose							
Canada Goose							

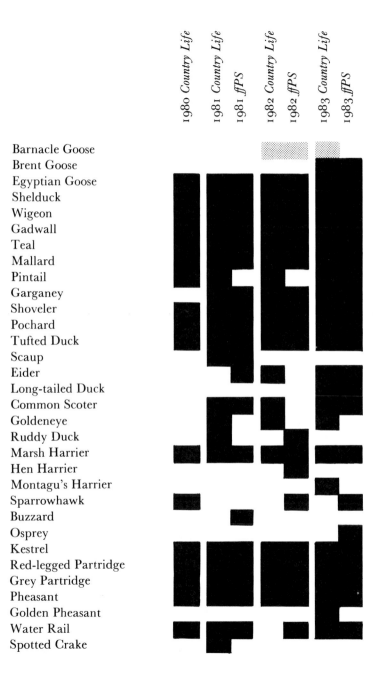

	1980 Country Life	1981 Country Life	1981 ffPS	1982 Country Life	1982 ffPS	1983 Country Life	1983 ffPS
Barnacle Goose							
Brent Goose							
Egyptian Goose							
Shelduck							
Wigeon							
Gadwall							
Teal							
Mallard							
Pintail							
Garganey							
Shoveler							
Pochard							
Tufted Duck							
Scaup							
Eider							
Long-tailed Duck							
Common Scoter							
Goldeneye							
Ruddy Duck							
Marsh Harrier							
Hen Harrier							
Montagu's Harrier							
Sparrowhawk							
Buzzard							
Osprey							
Kestrel							
Red-legged Partridge							
Grey Partridge							
Pheasant							
Golden Pheasant							
Water Rail							
Spotted Crake							

	1980 Country Life	1981 Country Life	1981 ffPS	1982 Country Life	1982 ffPS	1983 Country Life	1983 ffPS
Moorhen							
Coot							
Oystercatcher							
Avocet							
Stone Curlew							
Little Ringed Plover							
Ringed Plover							
Kentish Plover							
Dotterel							
Golden Plover					*		
Grey Plover							
Lapwing							
Knot							
Sanderling							
Little Stint							
Temminck's Stint							
Curlew Sandpiper							
Purple Sandpiper							
Dunlin							
Ruff							
Snipe							
Woodcock							
Black-tailed Godwit							
Bar-tailed Godwit							
Whimbrel							
Curlew							
Spotted Redshank							
Redshank							
Greenshank							
Green Sandpiper							
Wood Sandpiper							
Common Sandpiper							

Species	1980 Country Life	1981 Country Life	1981 ffPS	1982 Country Life	1982 ffPS	1983 Country Life	1983 ffPS
Turnstone	■	■		■	■	■	■
Mediterranean Gull	■			■	■		
Little Gull		■	■	■	■	■	■
Black-headed Gull	■	■	■	■	■	■	■
Common Gull	■	■	■	■	■	■	■
Lesser Black-backed Gull	■	■	■	■	■	■	■
Herring Gull	■	■	■	■	■	■	■
Iceland Gull	■	■	■	■			
Glaucous Gull	■			■	■		
Great Black-backed Gull	■	■	■	■	■	■	■
Kittiwake	■	■	■	■	■	■	■
Caspian Tern				■			
Sandwich Tern		■	■	■	■	■	■
Common Tern		■	■	■	■	■	■
Little Tern	■	■	■	■	■	■	■
Black Tern		■	■	■			
Guillemot		■	■				
Razorbill		■	■				
Feral Pigeon	■	■	■	■	■	■	■
Stock Dove	■	■	■	■	■	■	■
Woodpigeon	■	■	■	■	■	■	■
Collared Dove	■	■	■	■	■	■	■
Turtle Dove	■	■	■	■	■	■	■
Cuckoo	■	■	■	■	■	■	■
Barn Owl		■	■	■	■	■	■
Little Owl		■	■	■		■	■
Tawny Owl	■	■	■	■	■	■	■
Long-eared Owl	■	■	■	■		■	
Short-eared Owl	■	■		■	■		■
Nightjar				■	■		
Swift				■	■	■	■
Kingfisher	■	■	■	■	■	■	■

1980 *Country Life*
1981 *Country Life*
1981 *ffPS*
1982 *Country Life*
1982 *ffPS*
1983 *Country Life*
1983 *ffPS*

Green Woodpecker
Great Spotted Woodpecker
Lesser Spotted Woodpecker
Woodlark
Skylark
Sand Martin
Swallow
House Martin
Tree Pipit
Meadow Pipit
Yellow Wagtail
Grey Wagtail
Pied Wagtail
Wren
Dunnock
Robin
Nightingale
Black Redstart
Redstart
Whinchat
Stonechat
Wheatear
Ring Ousel
Blackbird
Fieldfare
Song Thrush
Redwing
Mistle Thrush
Cetti's Warbler
Grasshopper Warbler
Savi's Warbler
Sedge Warbler

	1980 Country Life	1981 Country Life	1981 ffPS	1982 Country Life	1982 ffPS	1983 Country Life	1983 ffPS

Reed Warbler
Lesser Whitethroat
Whitethroat
Garden Warbler
Blackcap
Wood Warbler
Chiffchaff
Willow Warbler
Goldcrest
Firecrest
Spotted Flycatcher
Pied Flycatcher
Bearded Tit
Long-tailed Tit
Marsh Tit
Willow Tit
Coal Tit
Blue Tit
Great Tit
Nuthatch
Treecreeper
Red-backed Shrike
Jay
Magpie
Jackdaw
Rook
Carrion Crow
Starling
House Sparrow
Tree Sparrow
Chaffinch
Brambling

Greenfinch
Goldfinch
Siskin
Linnet
Redpoll
Common Crossbill
Bullfinch
Hawfinch
Yellowhammer
Reed Bunting
Corn Bunting

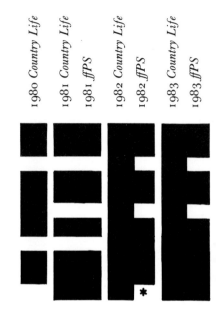